MW01332154

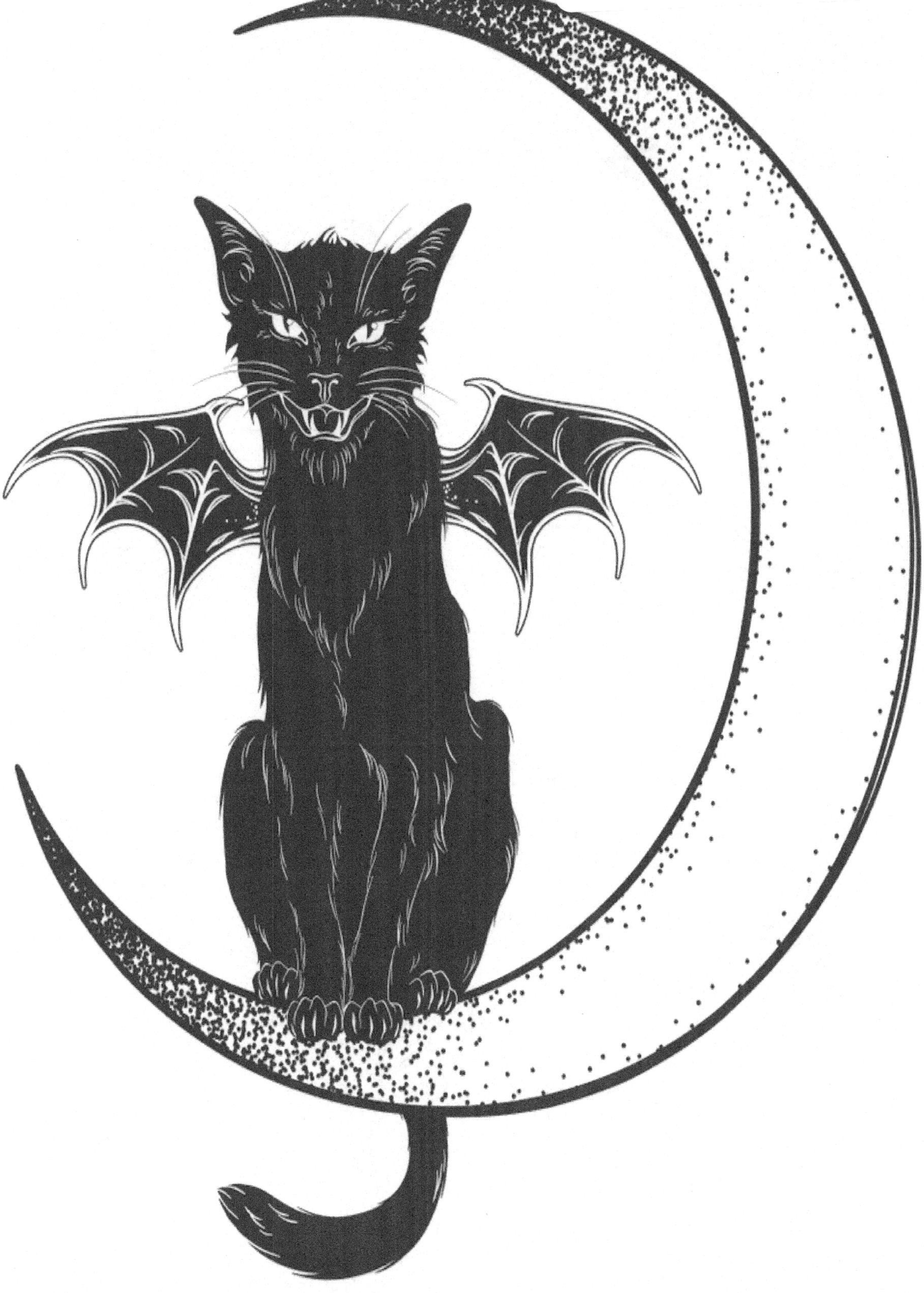

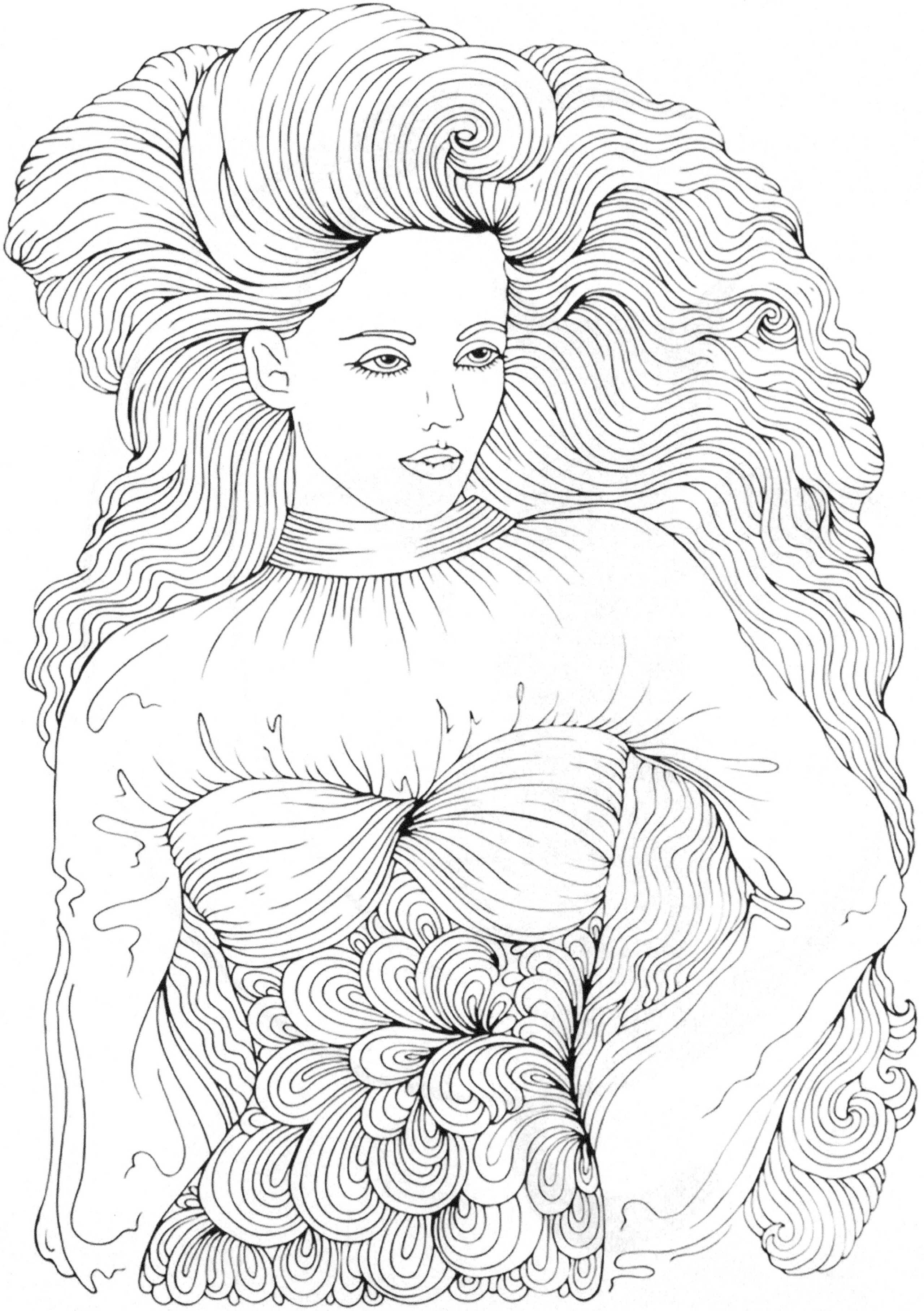

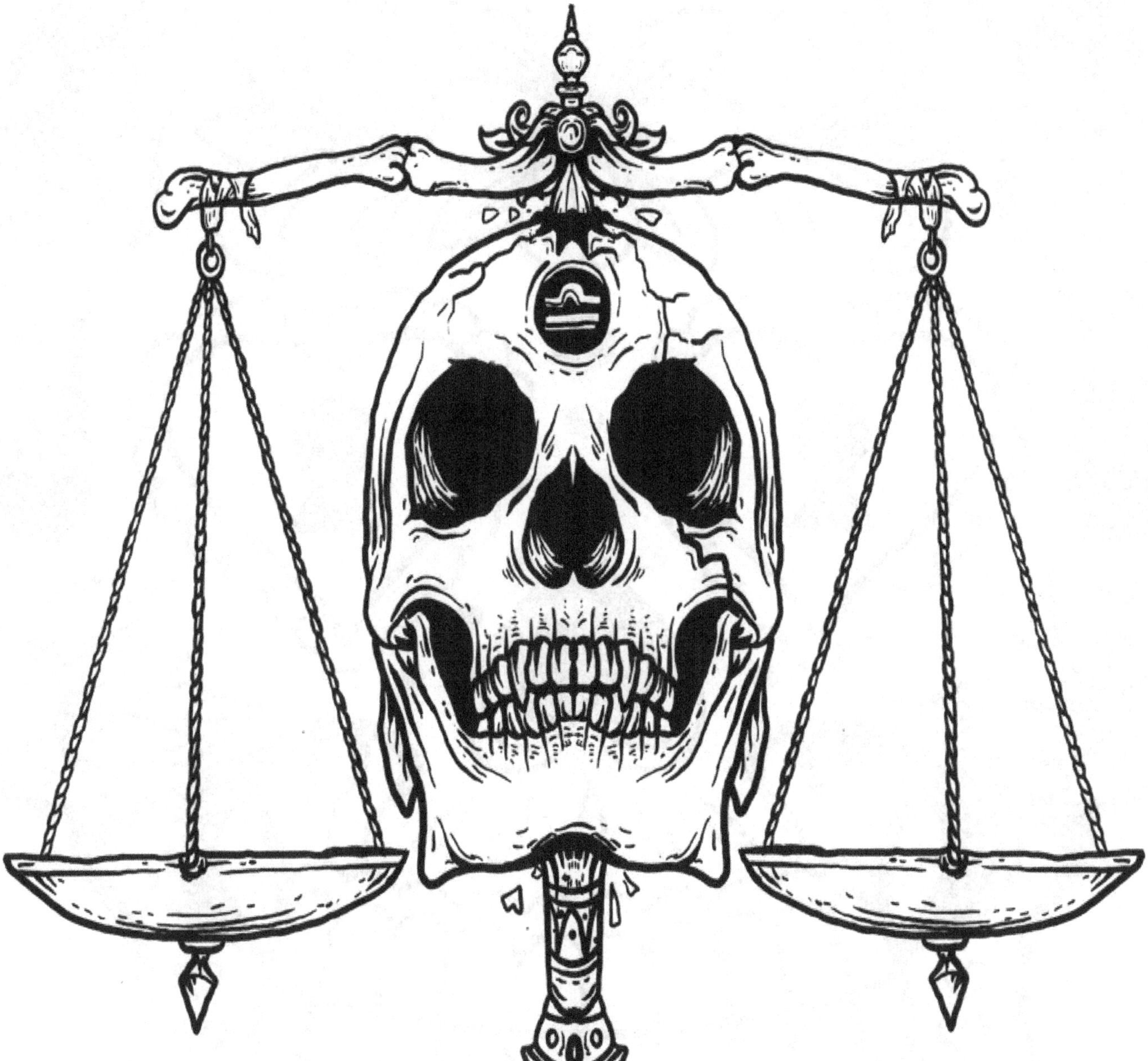

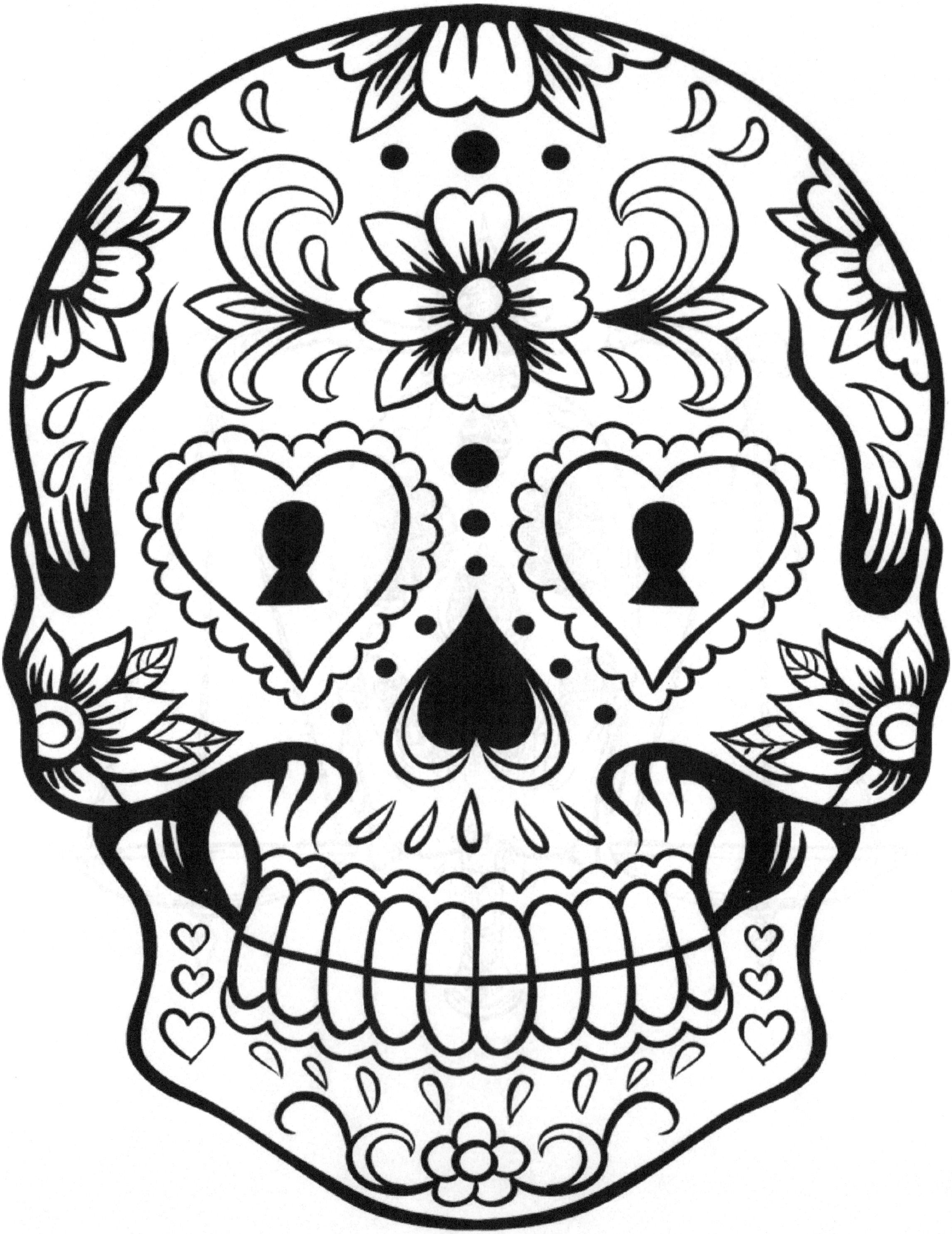

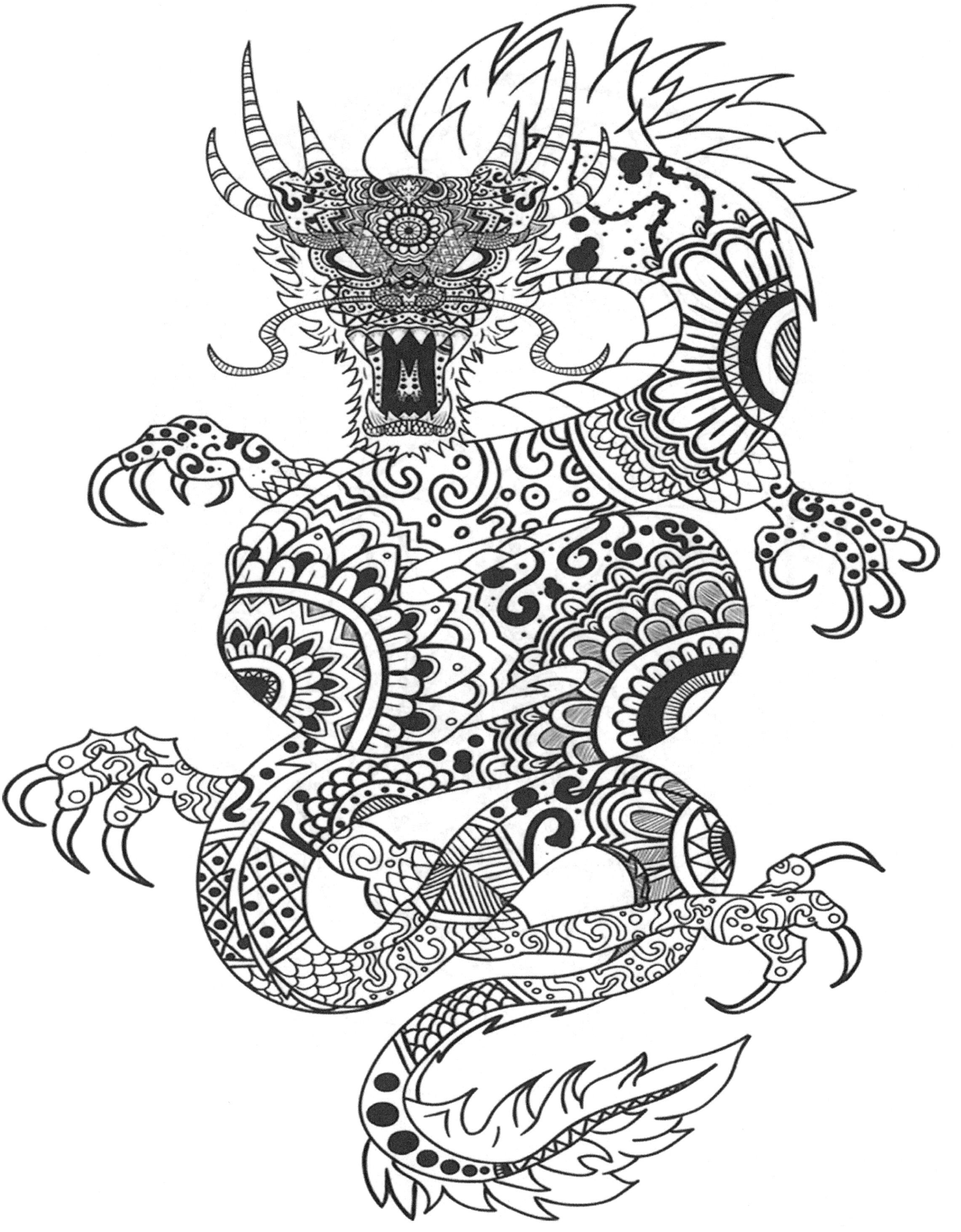

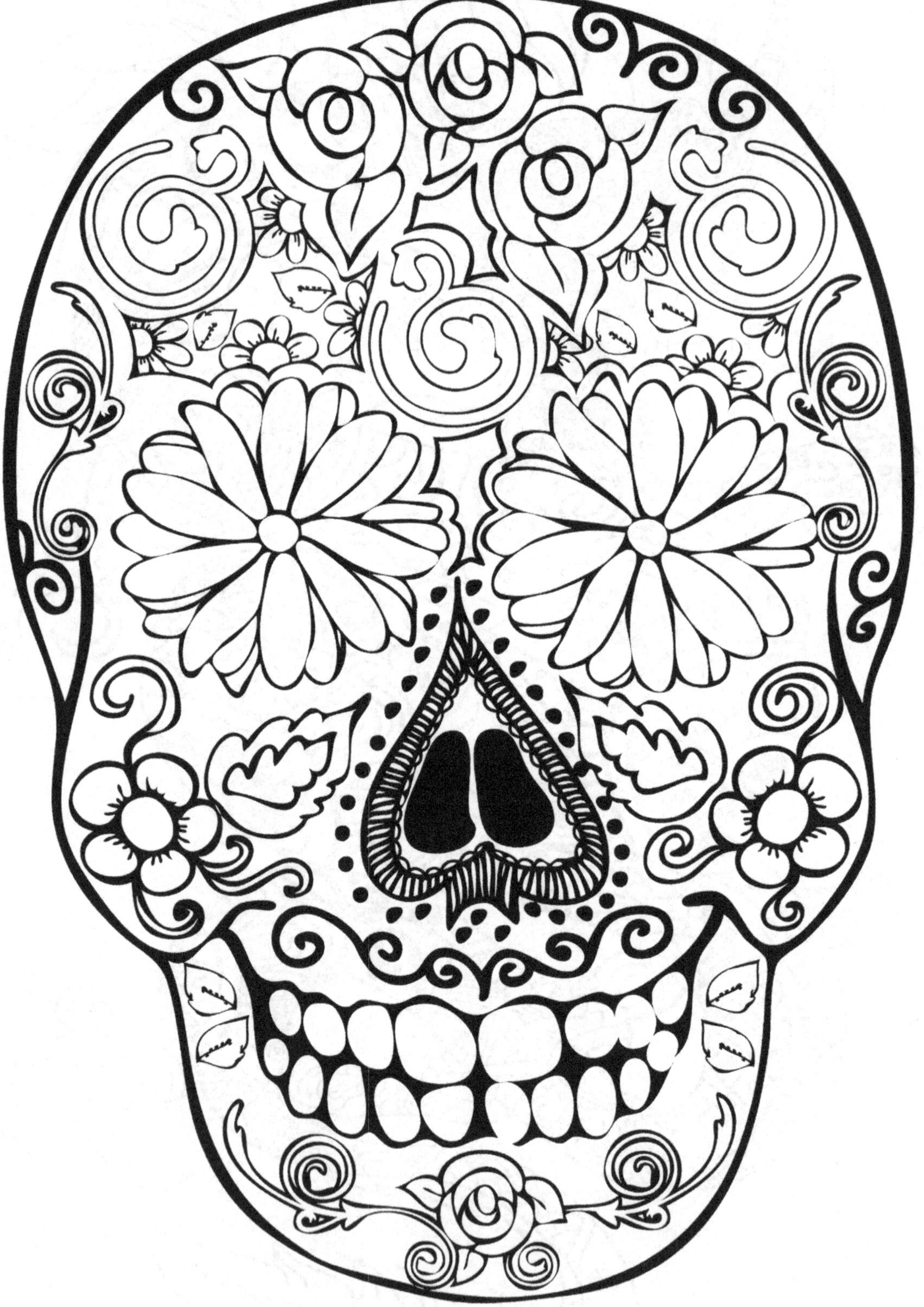

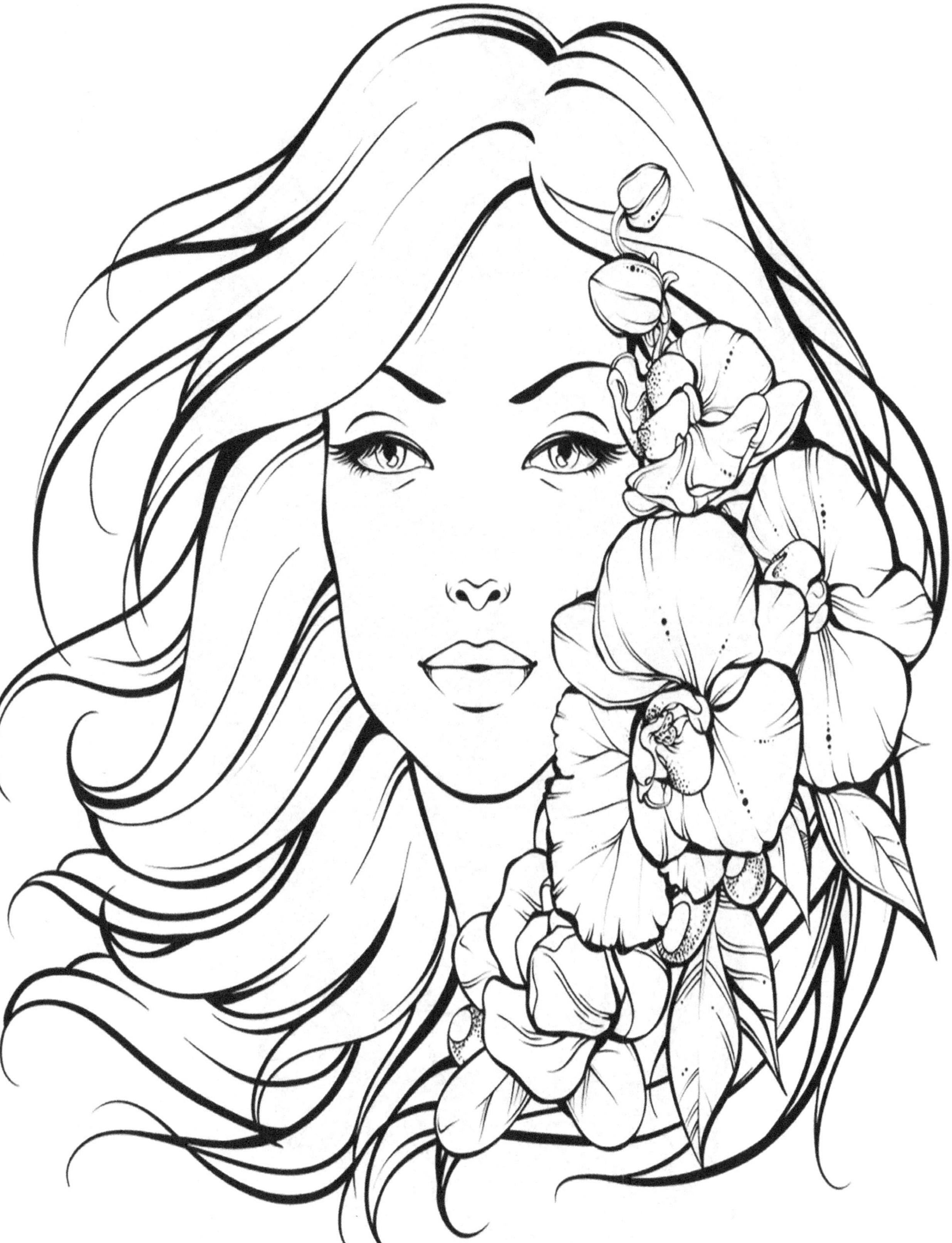

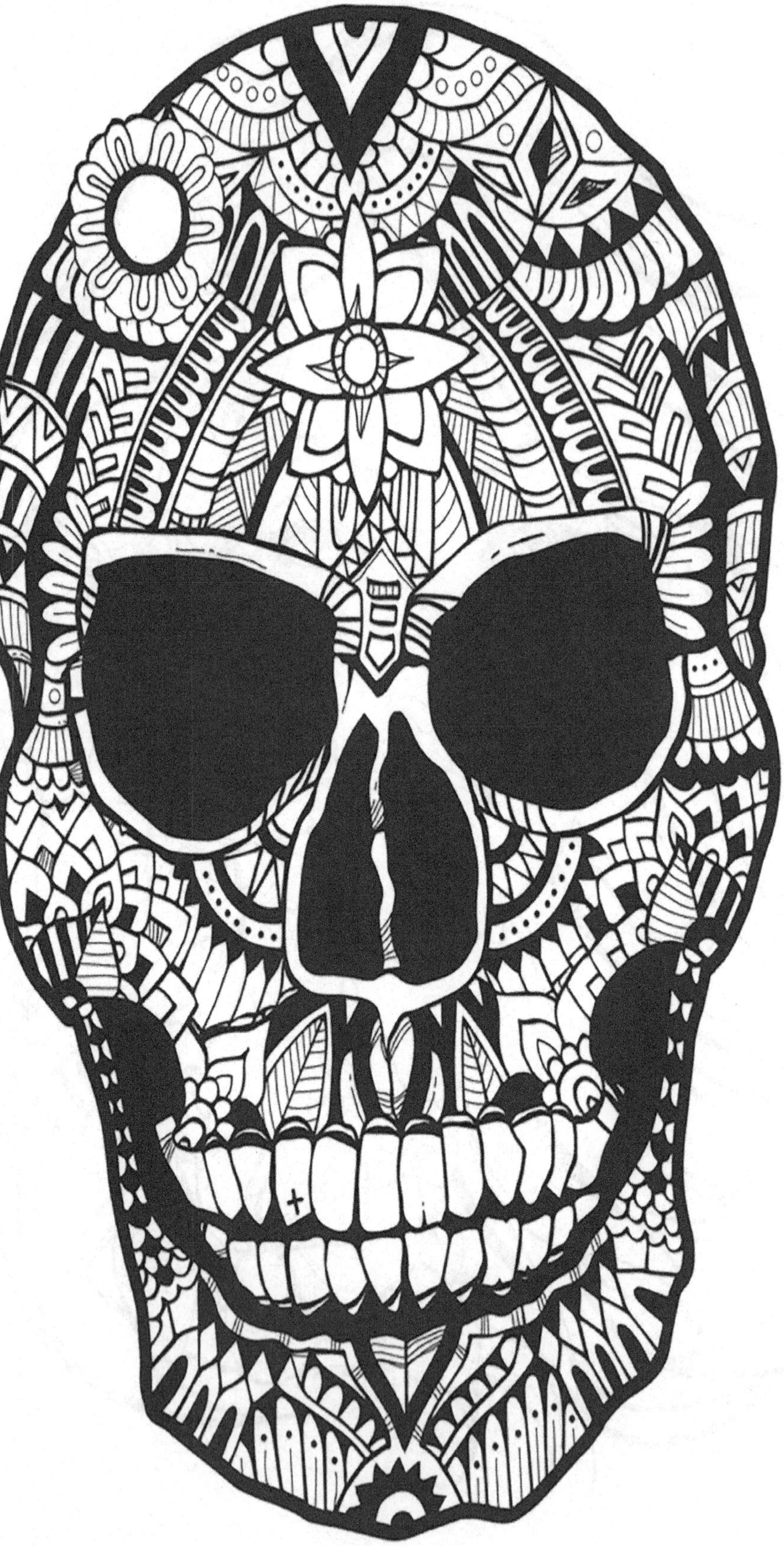

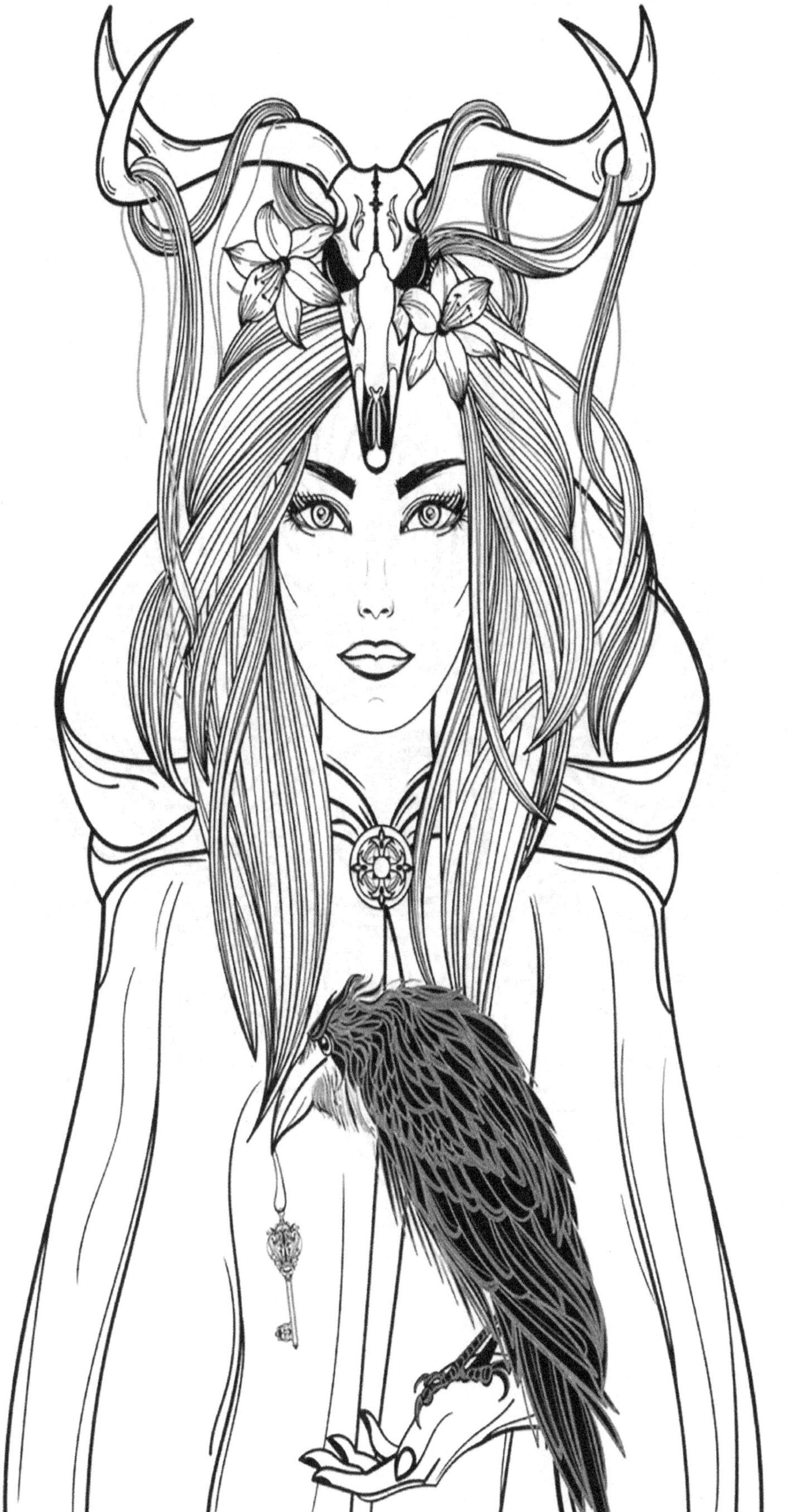

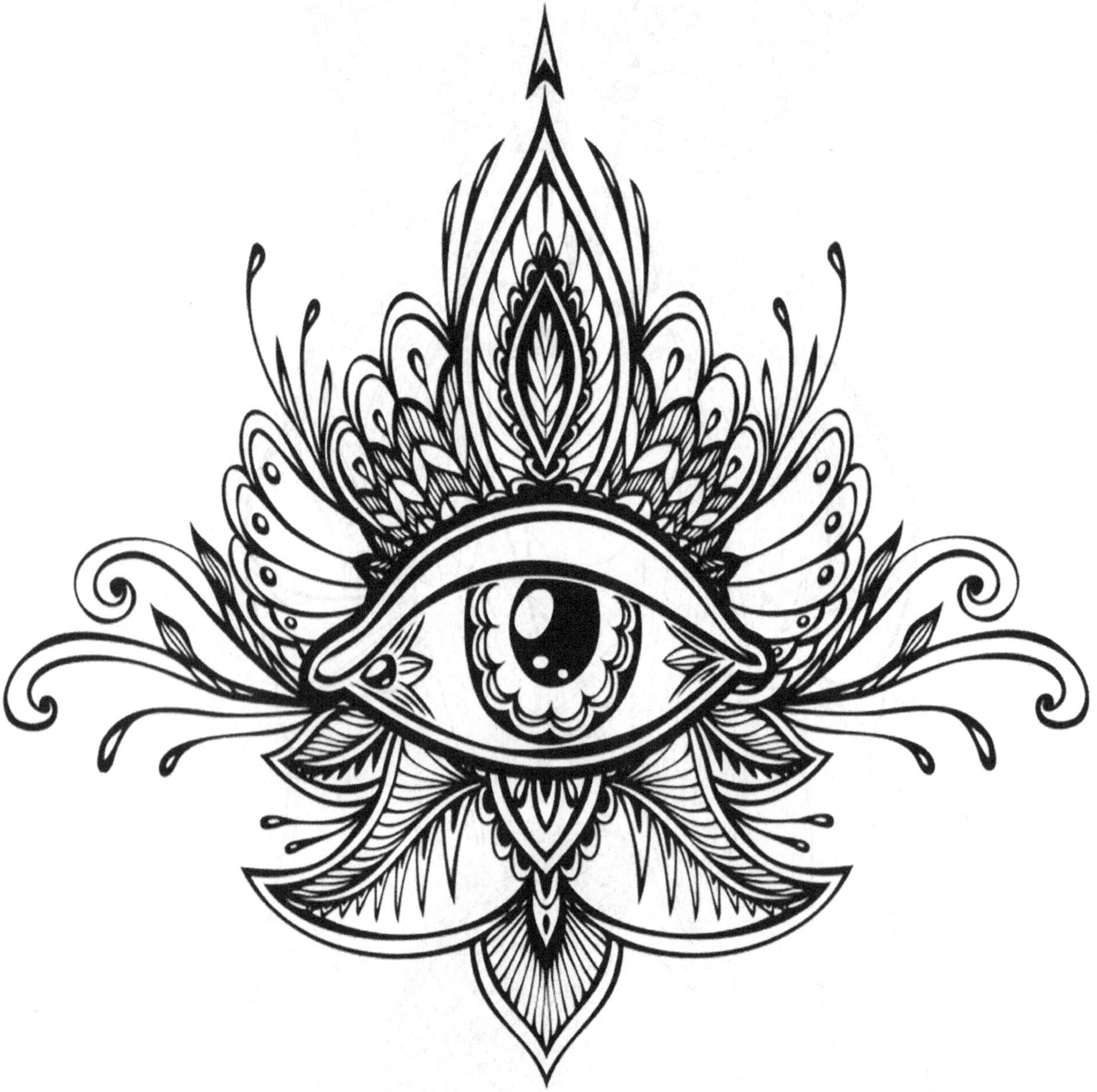

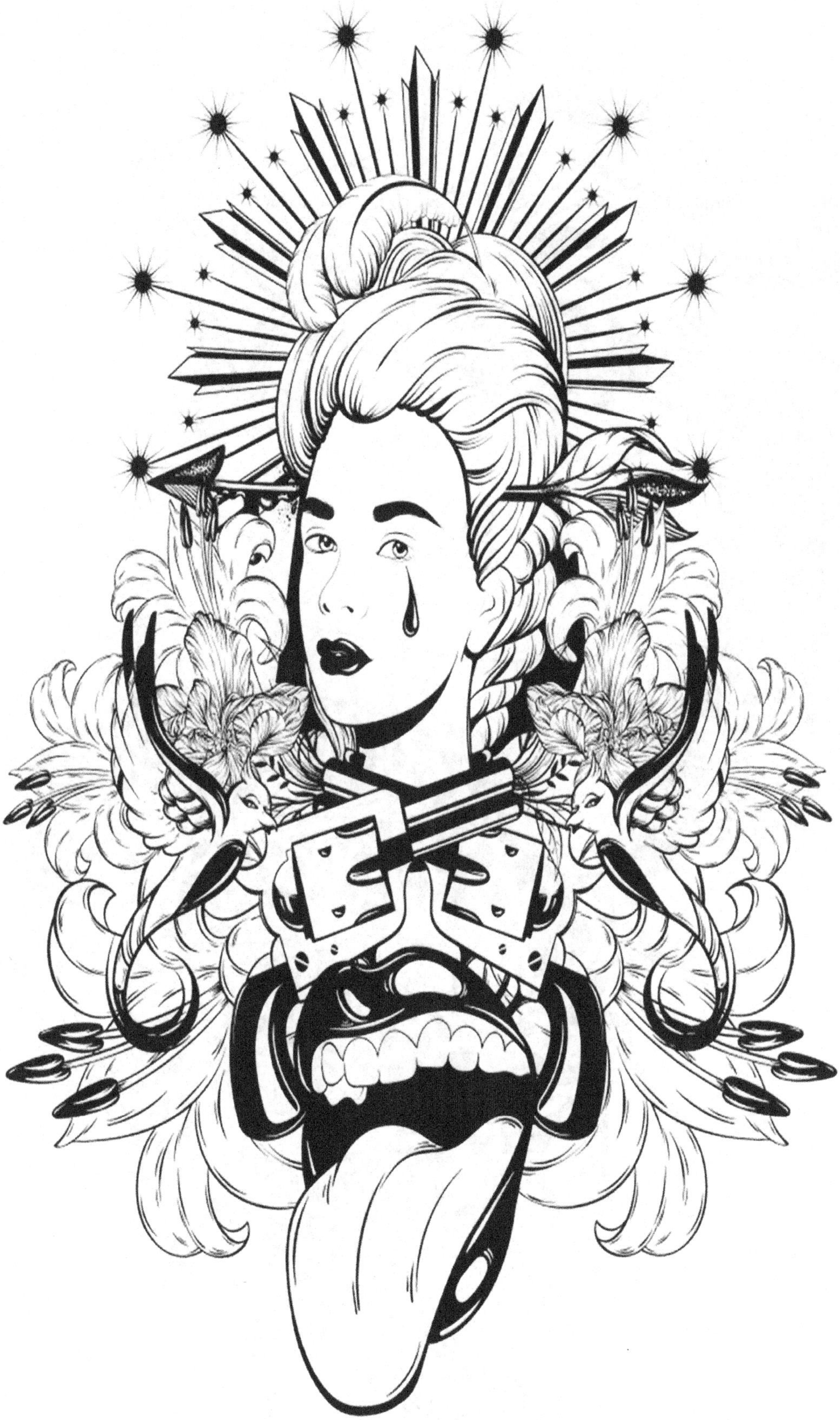

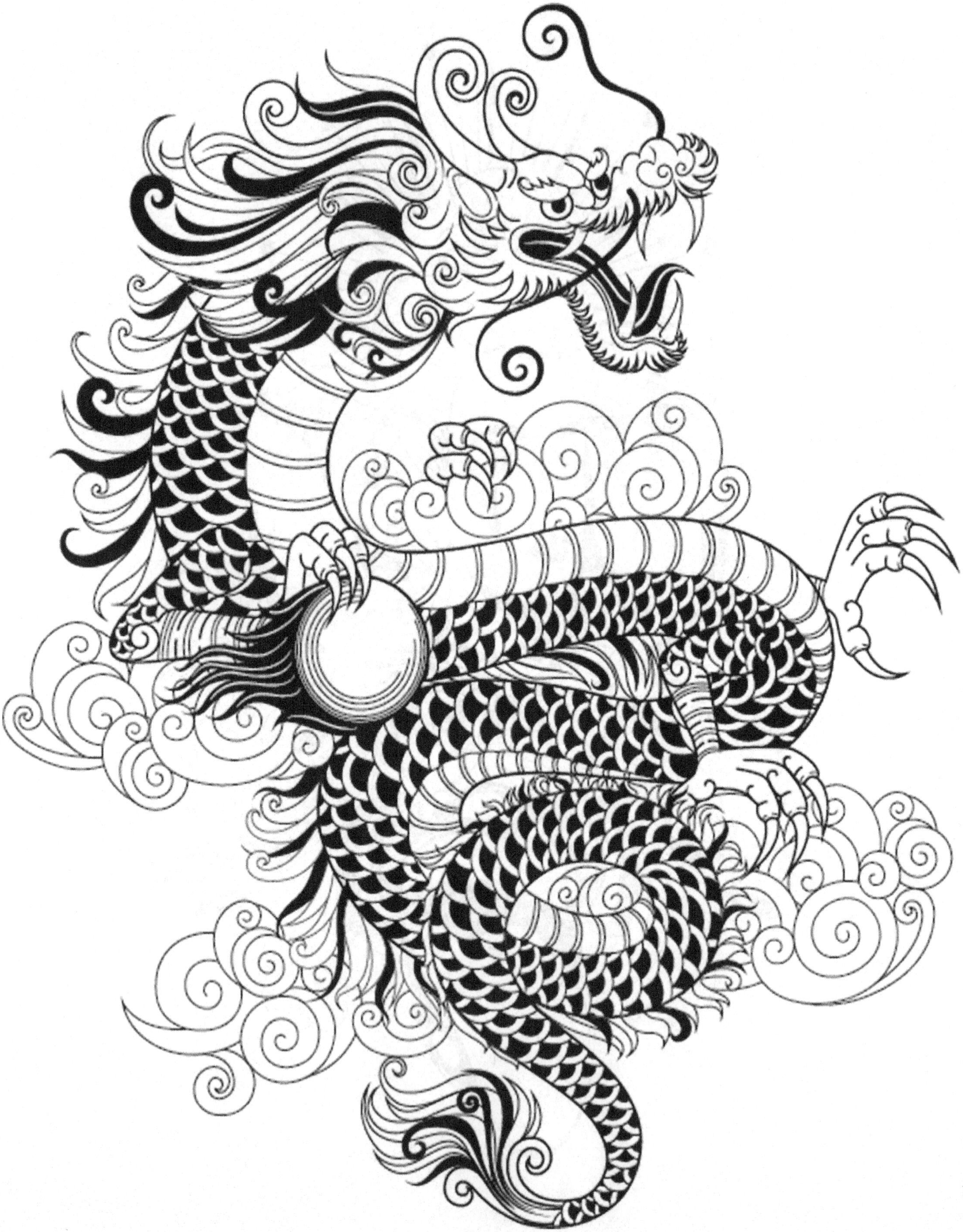

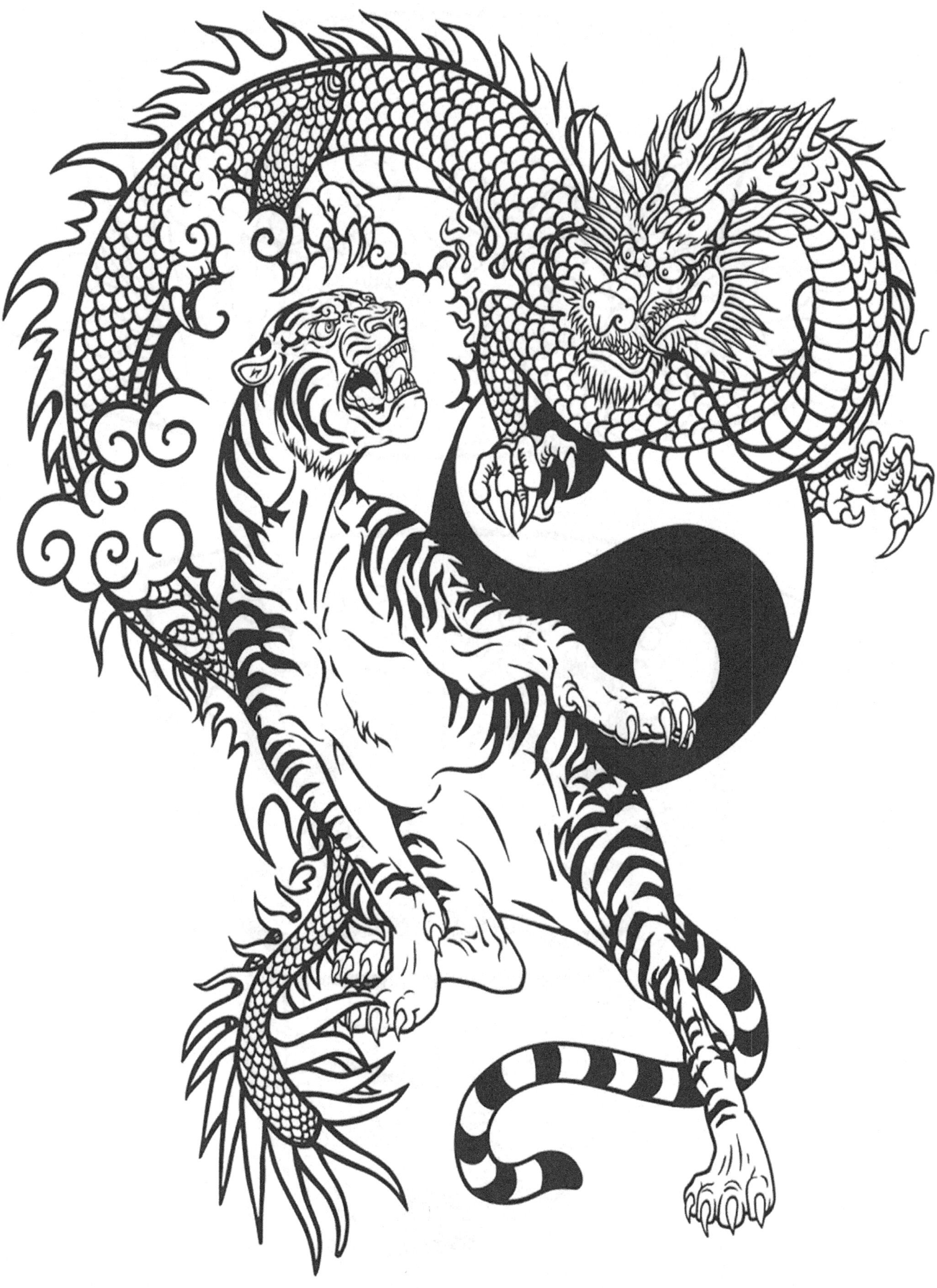

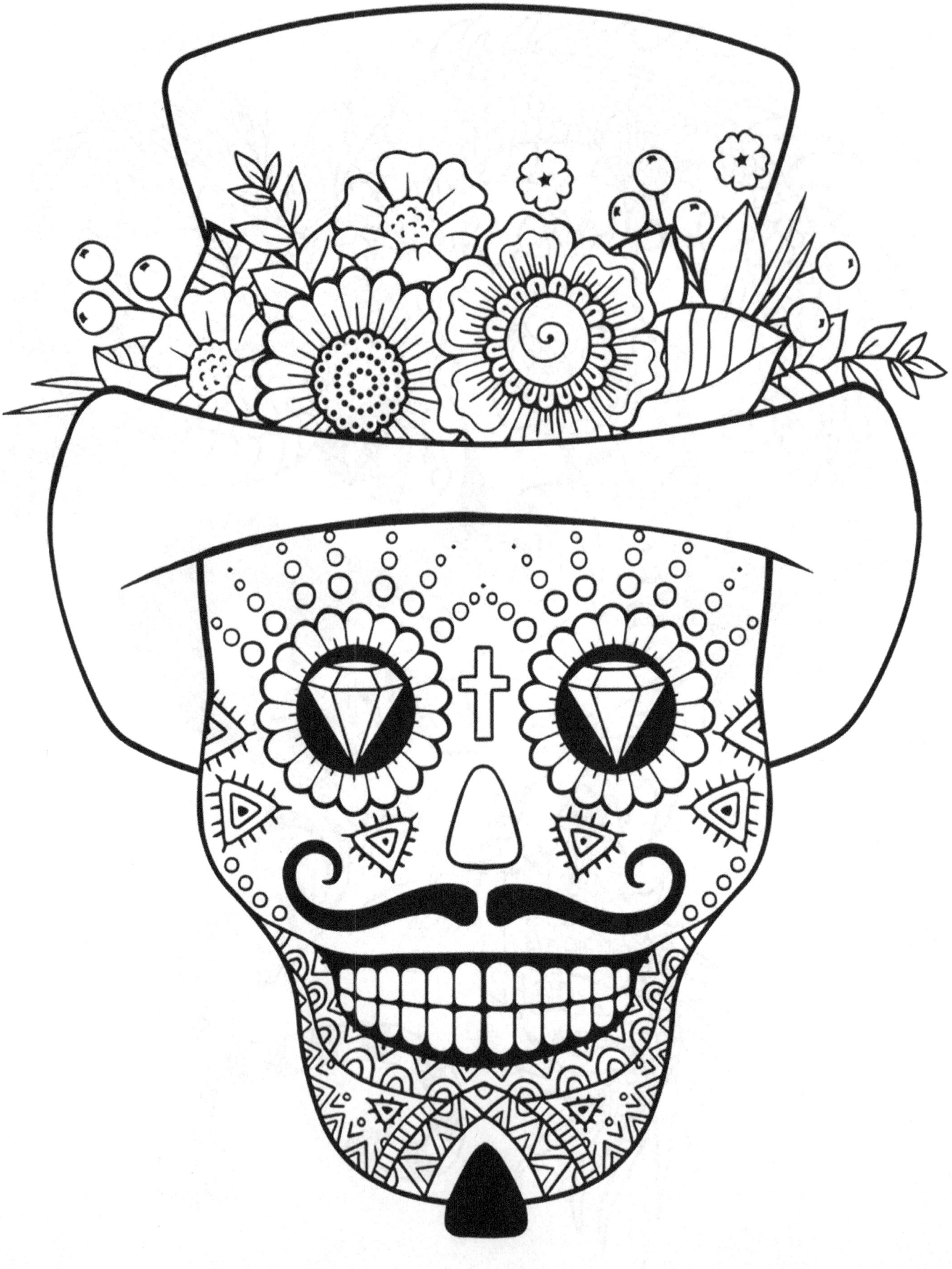

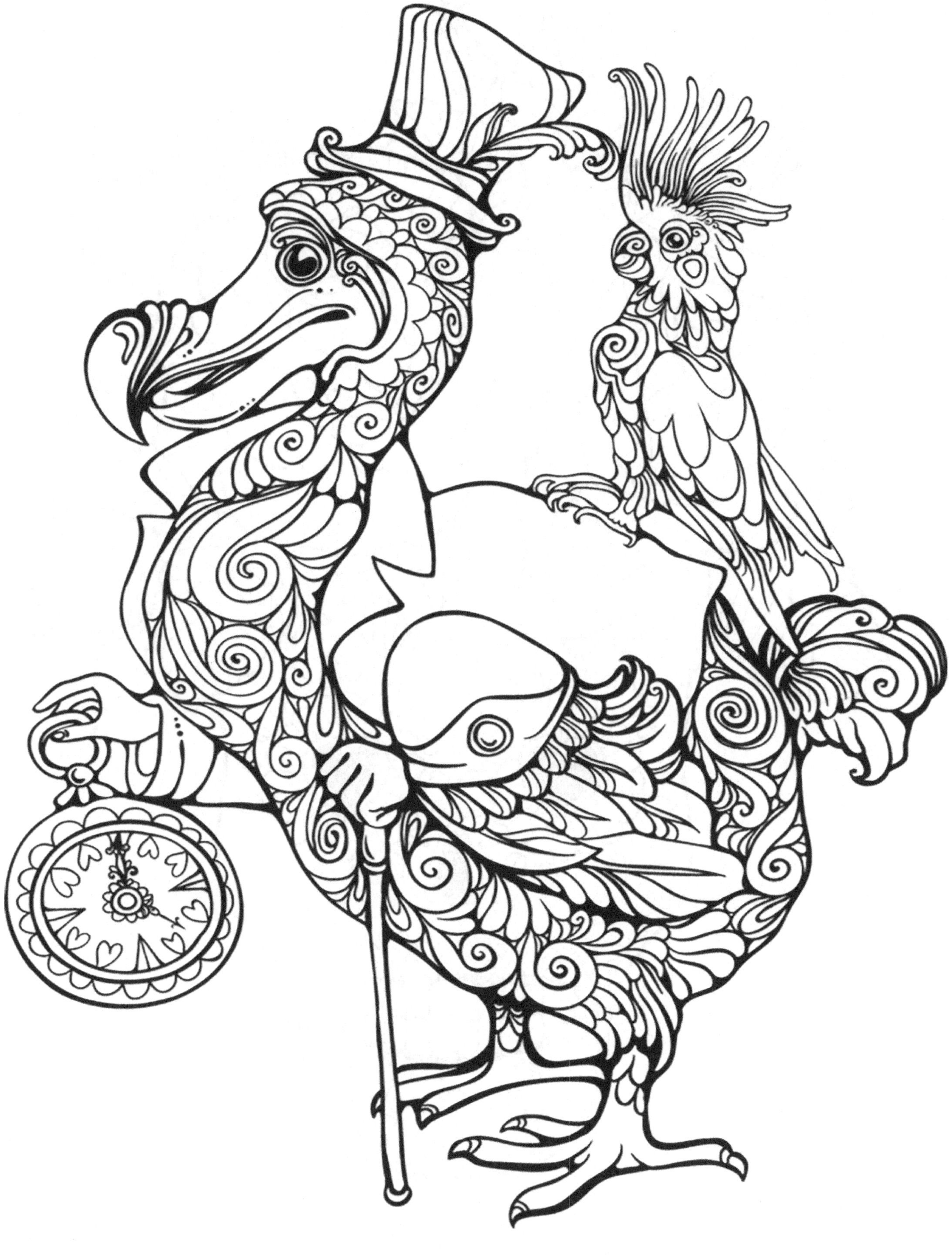

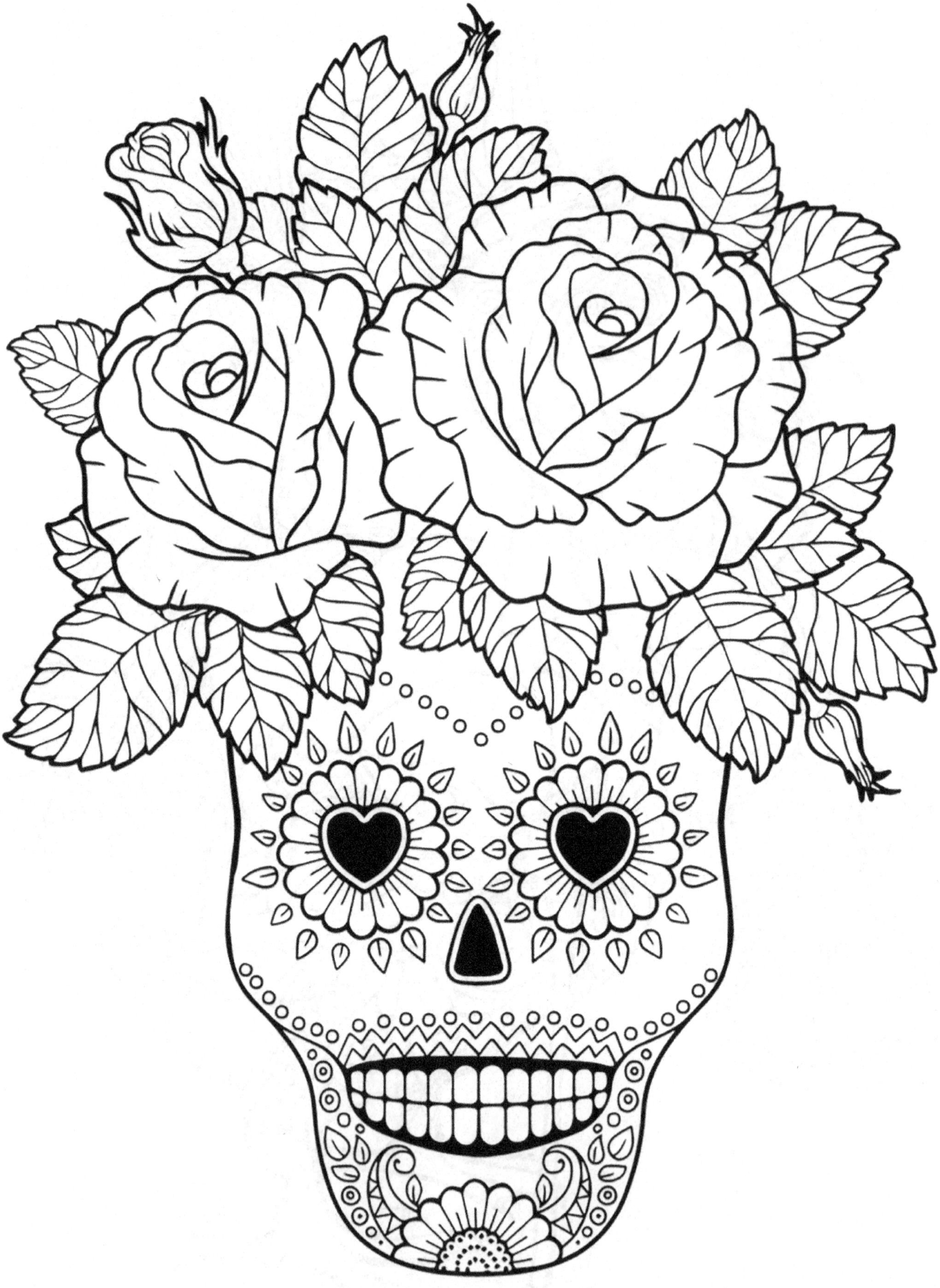

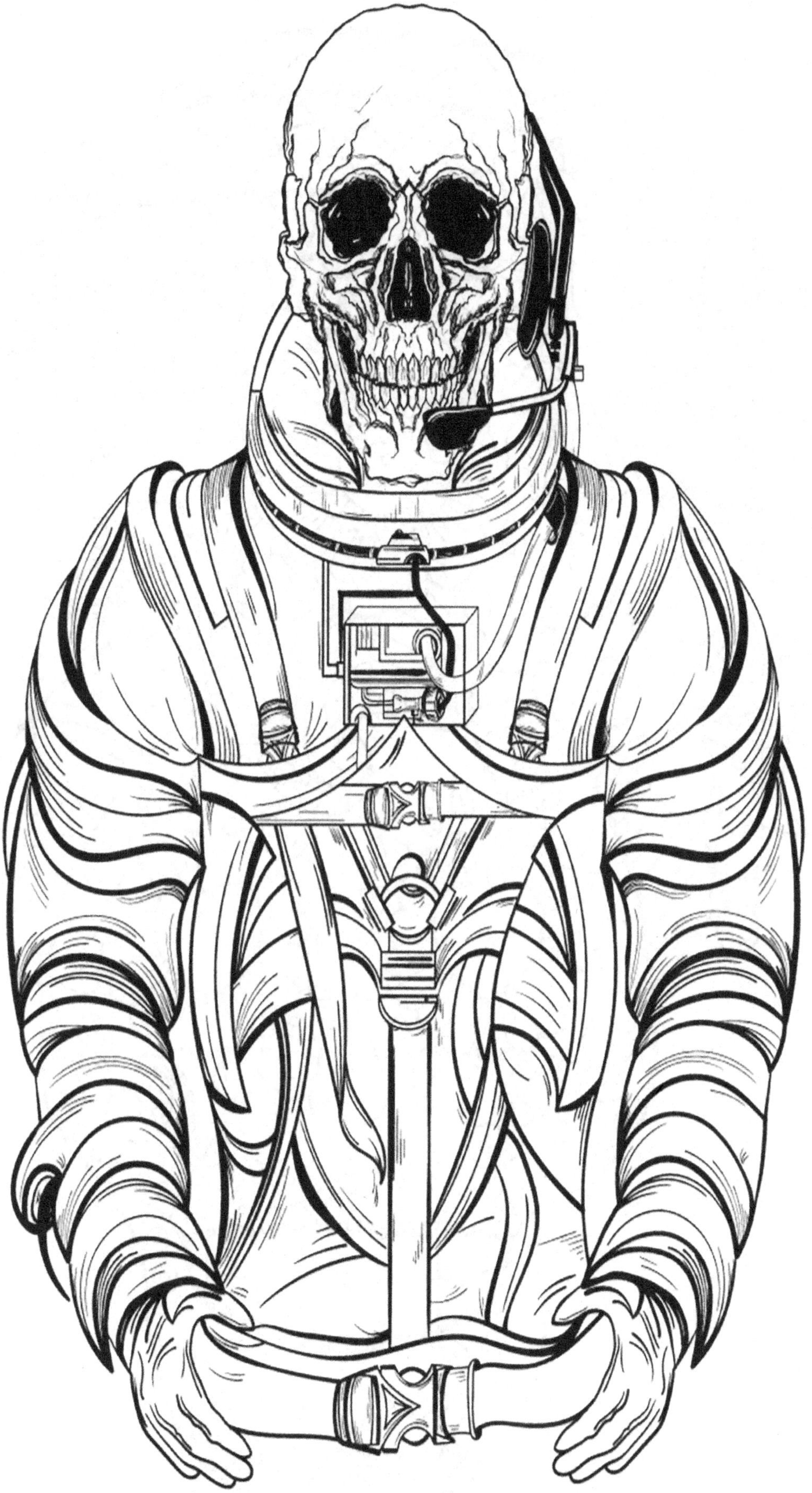

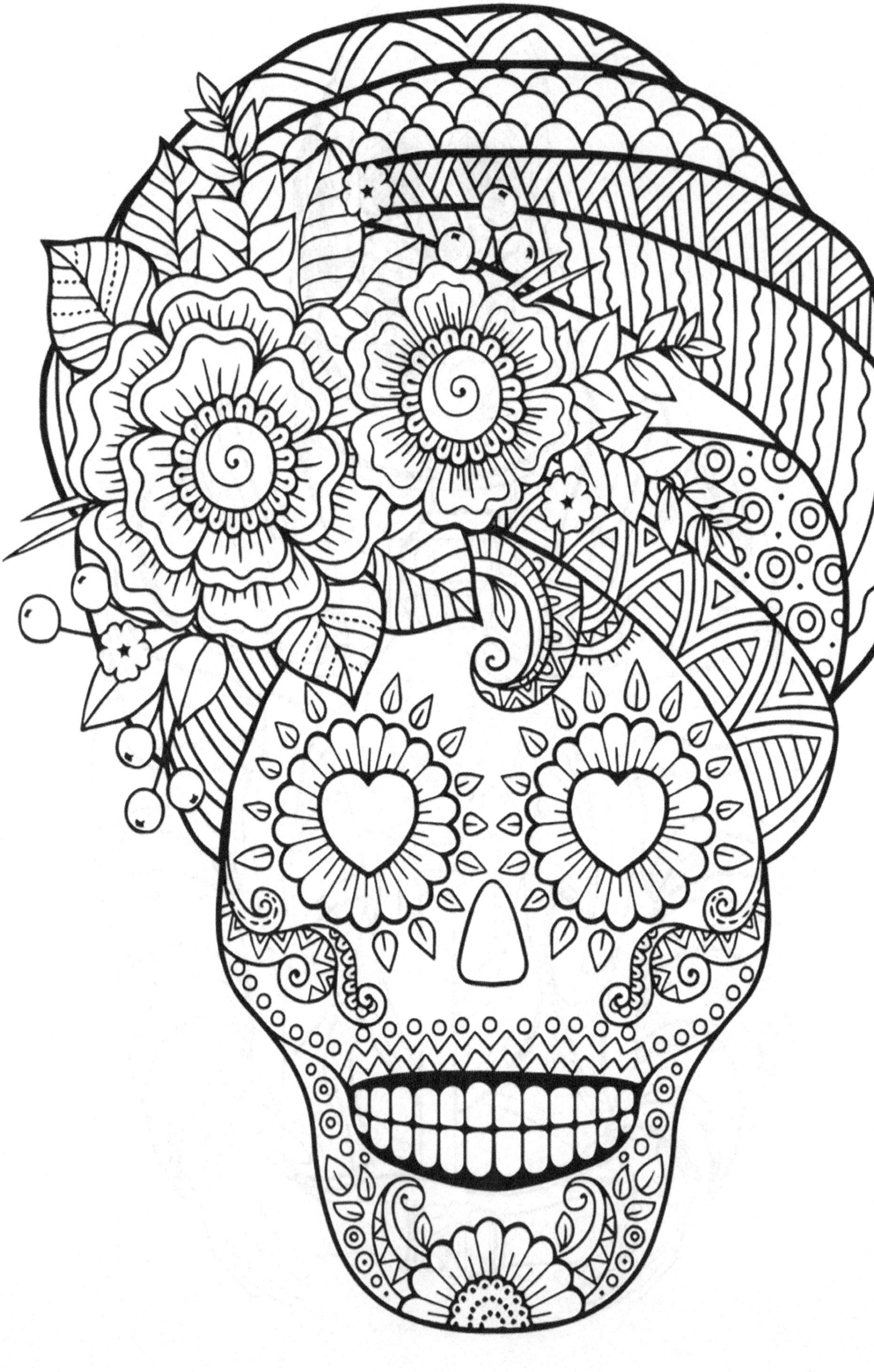

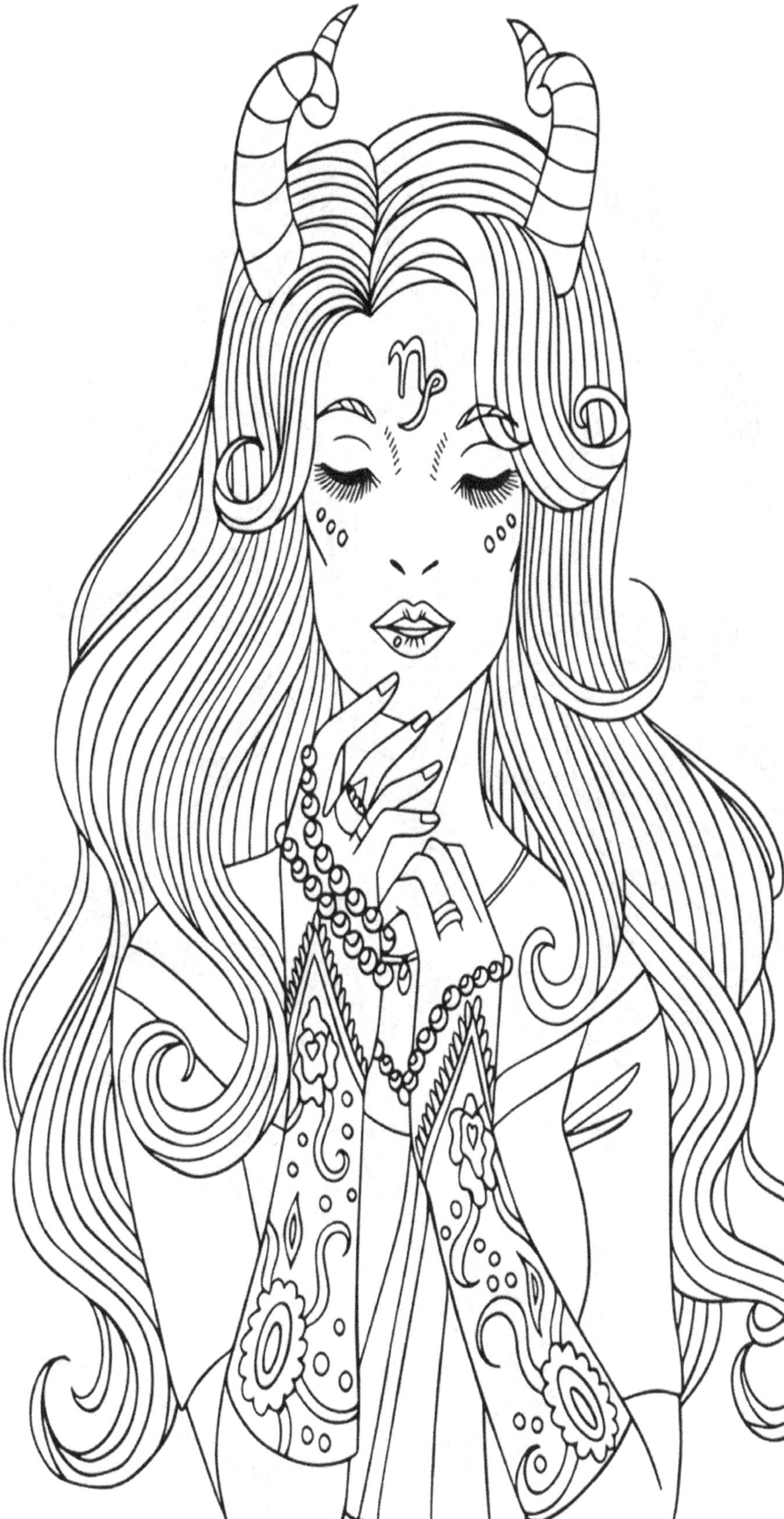

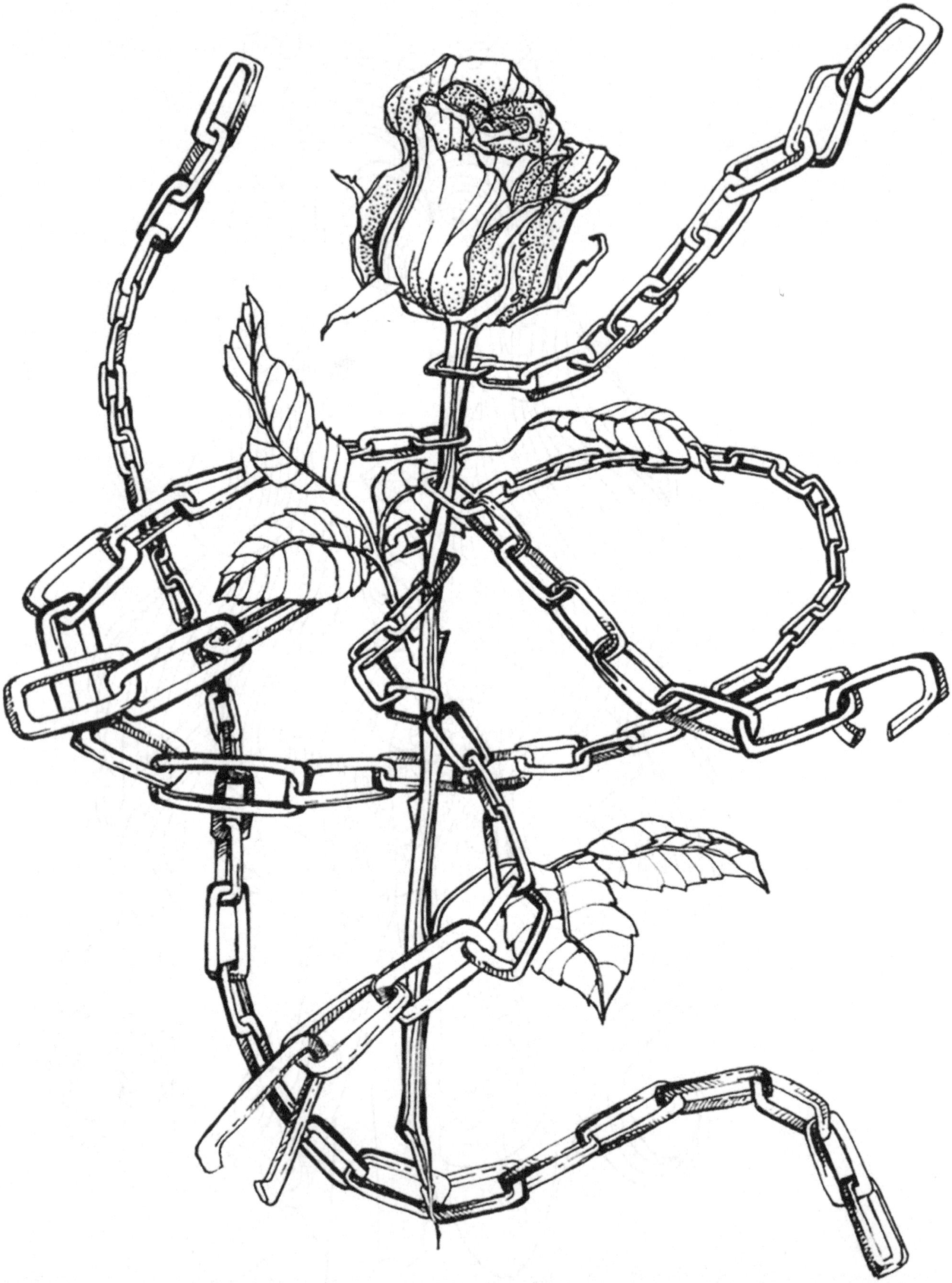

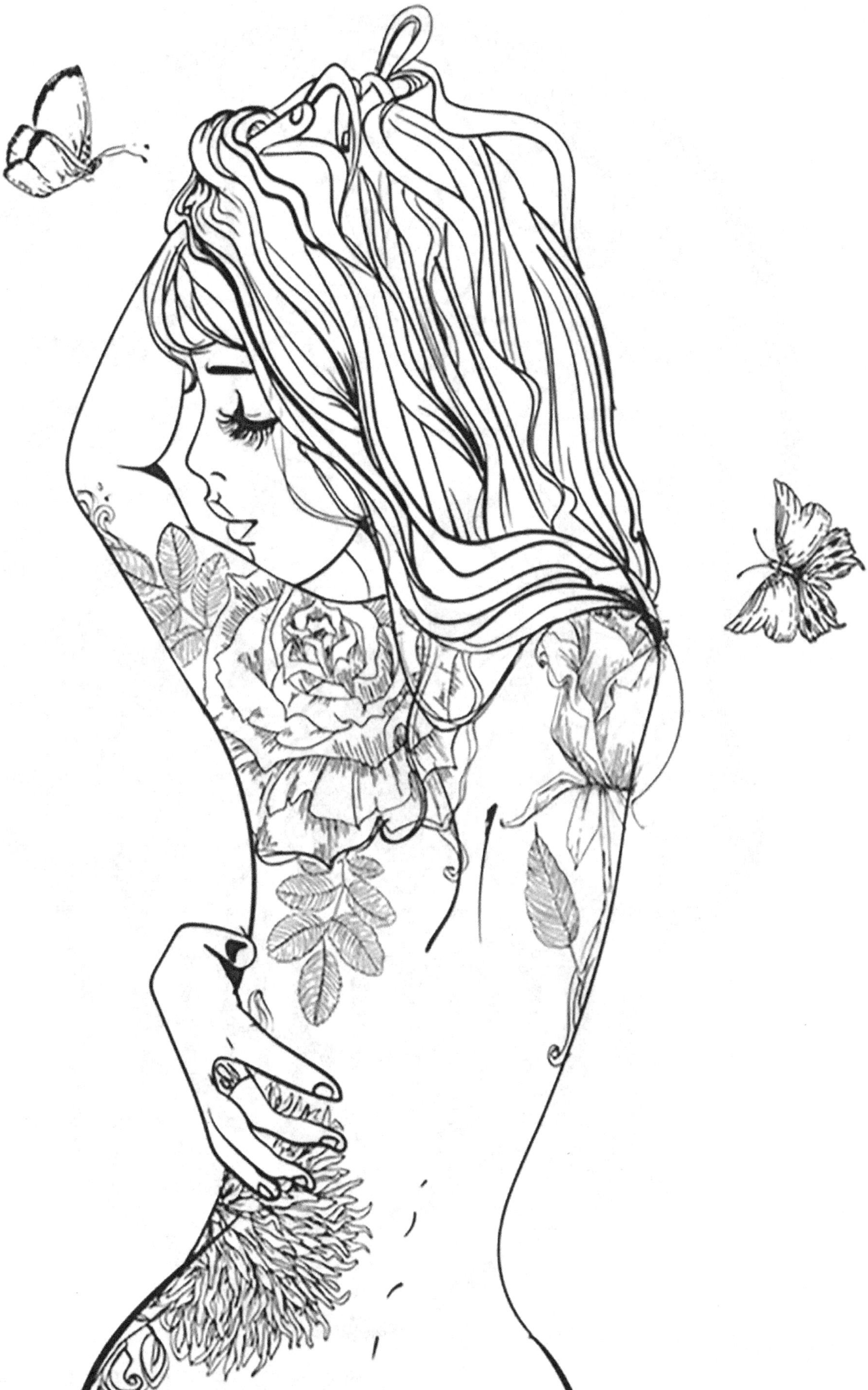

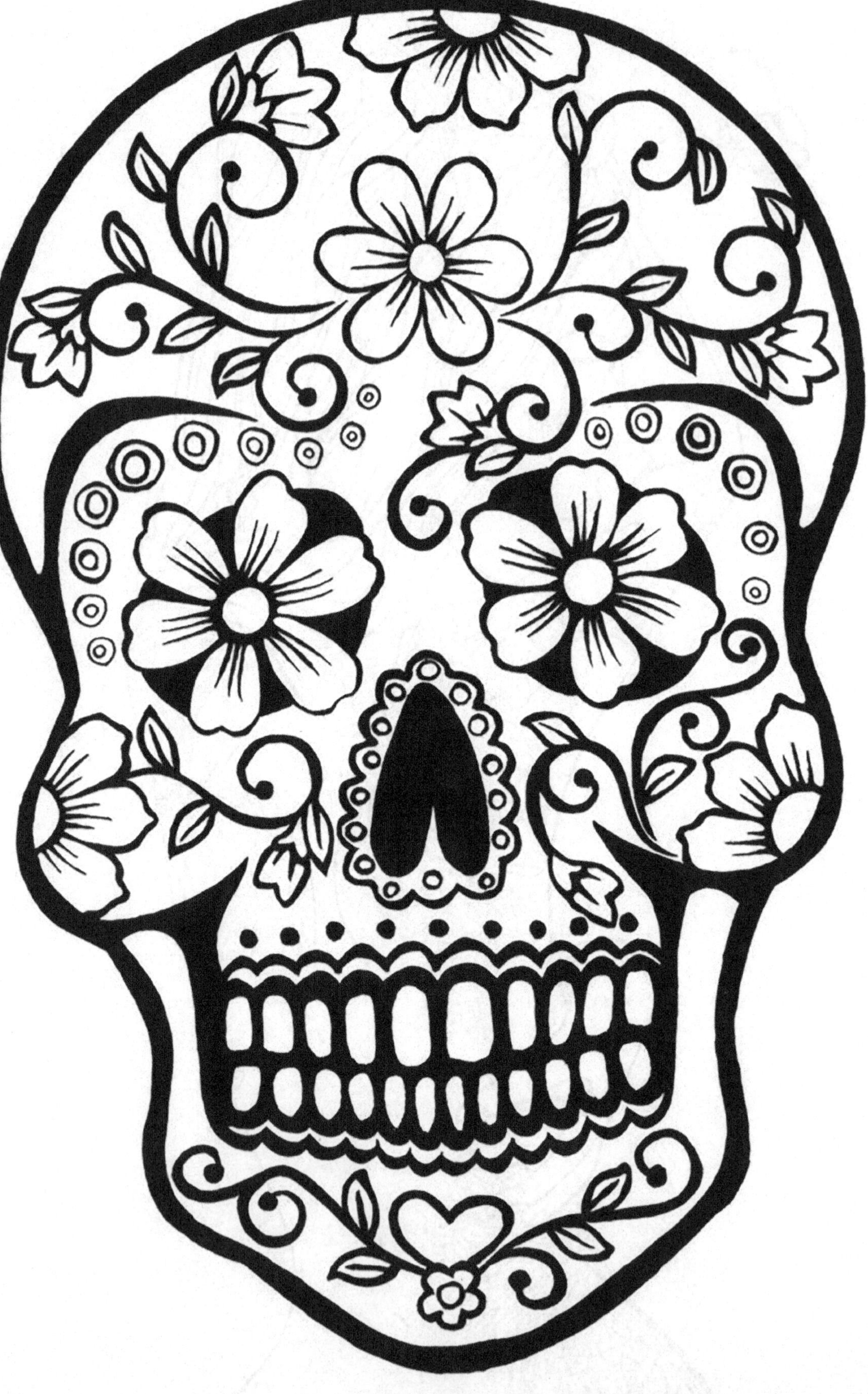

PESCNO.BLOGSPOT.COM

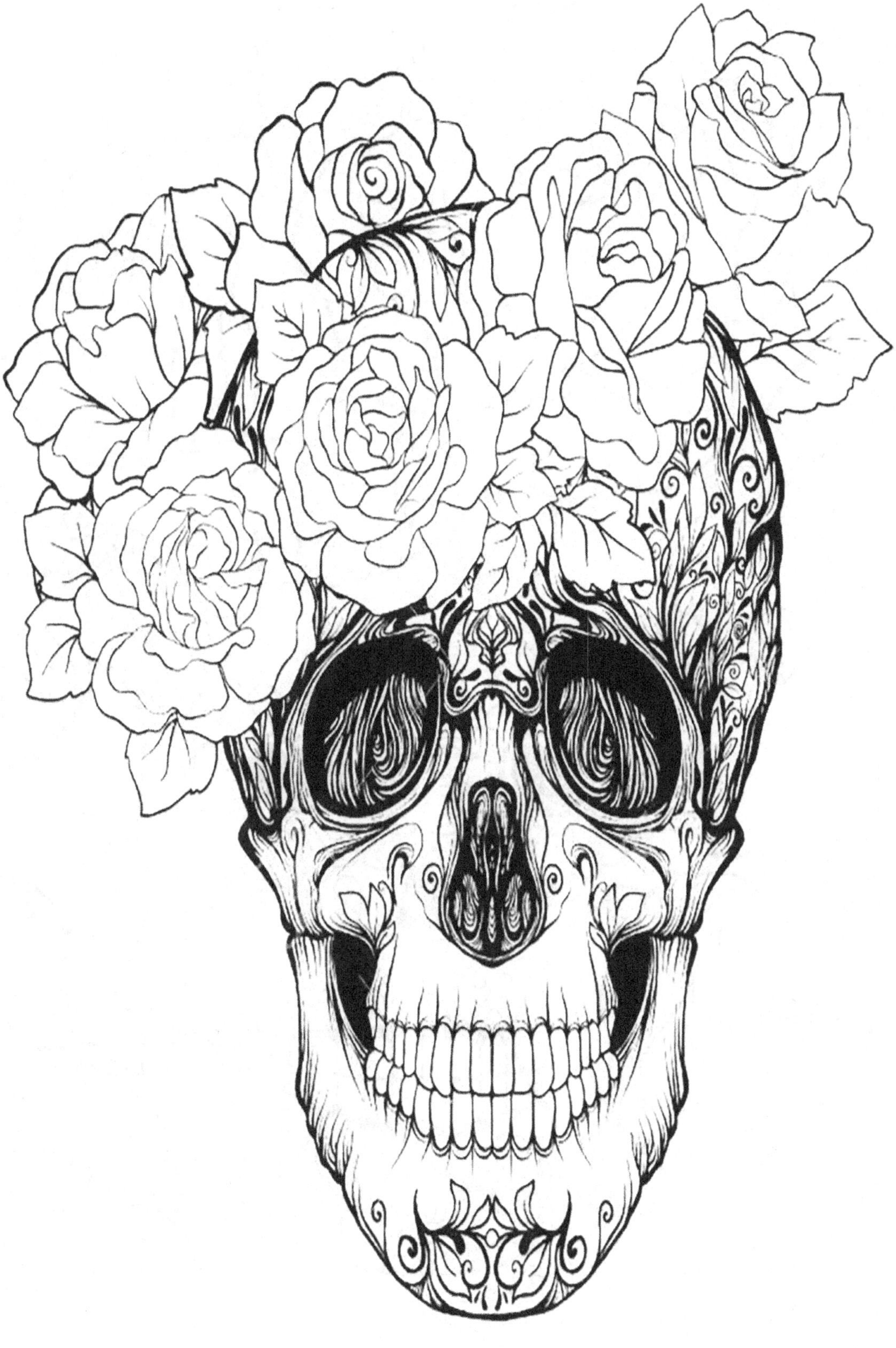

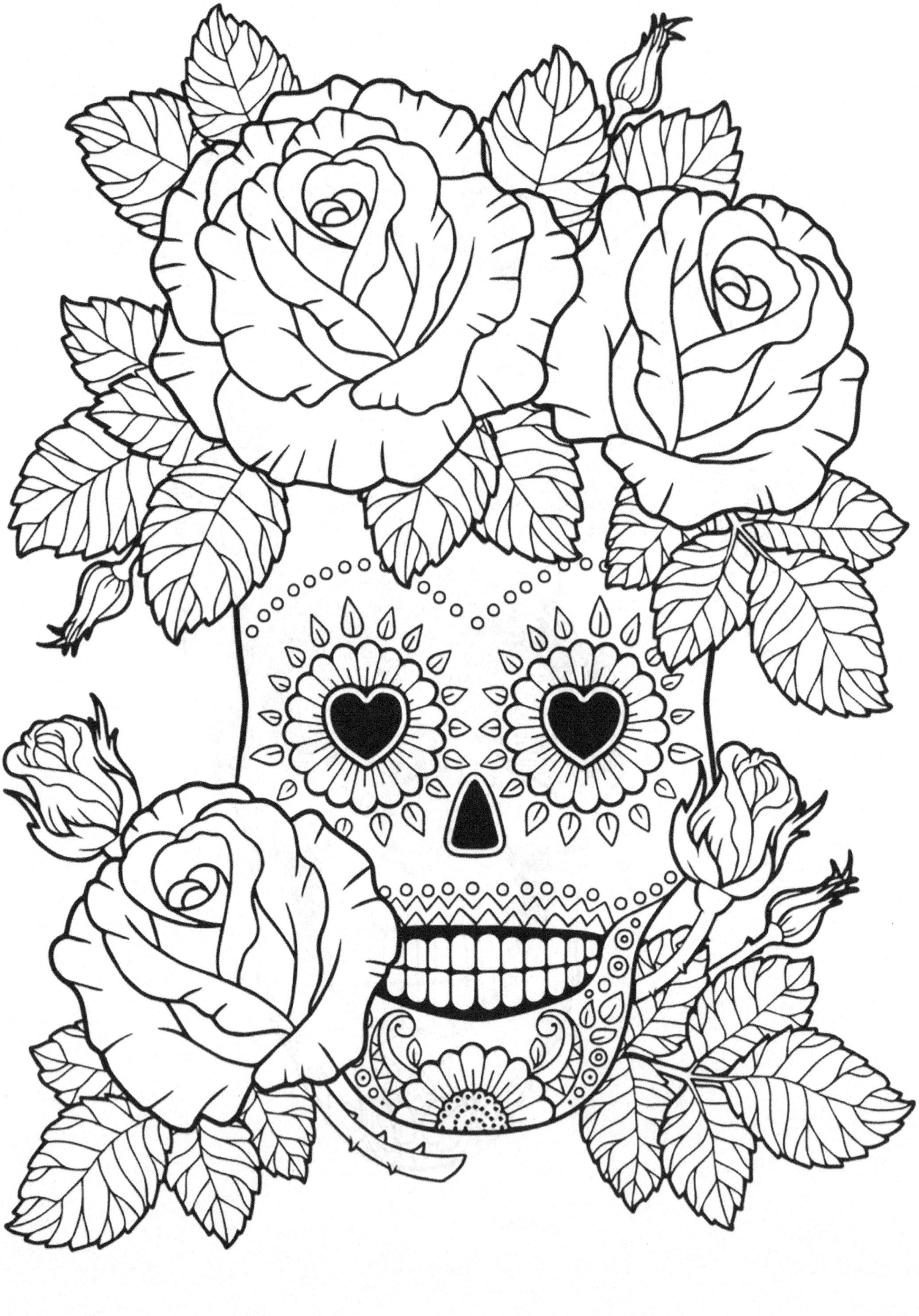

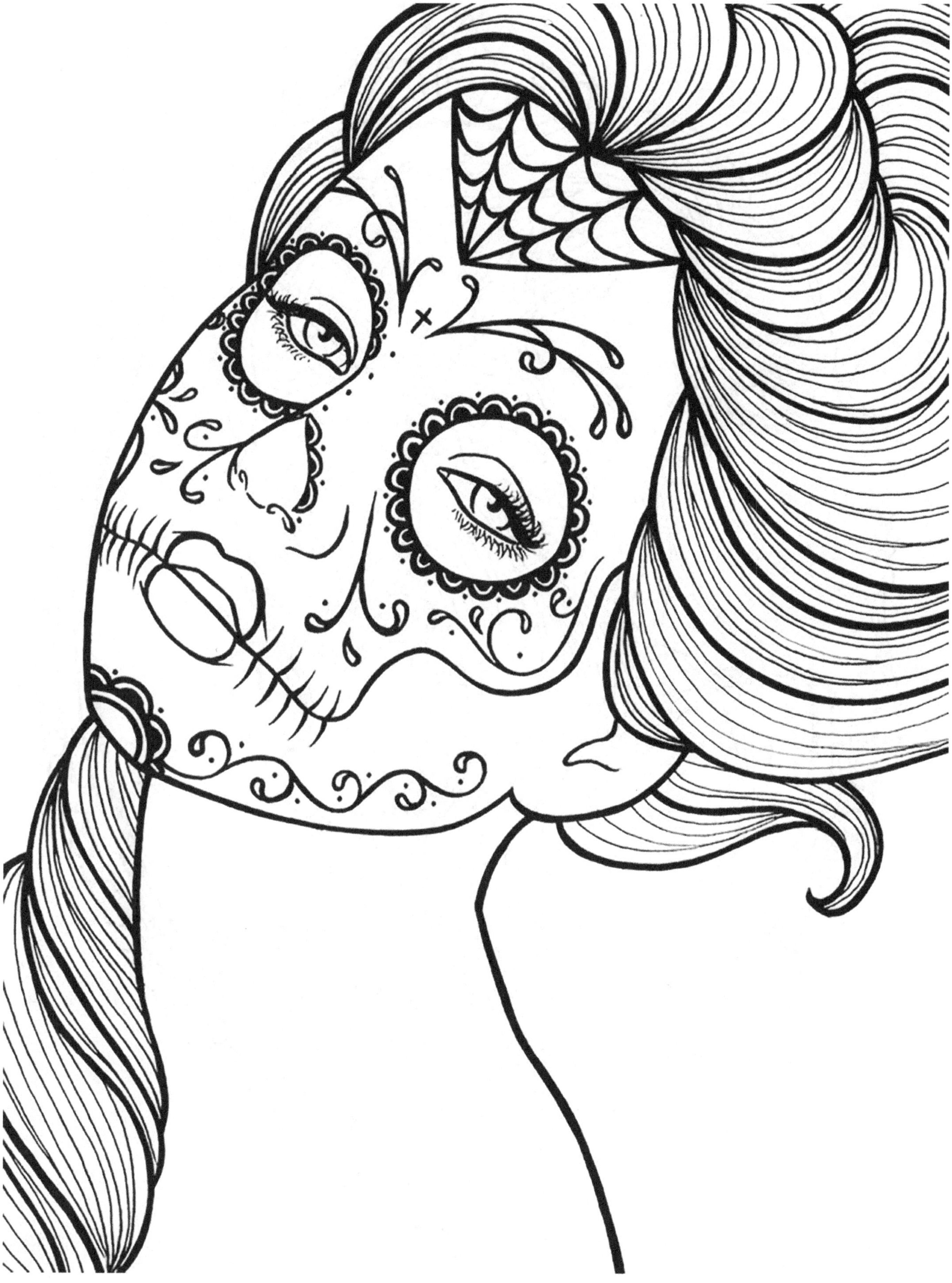

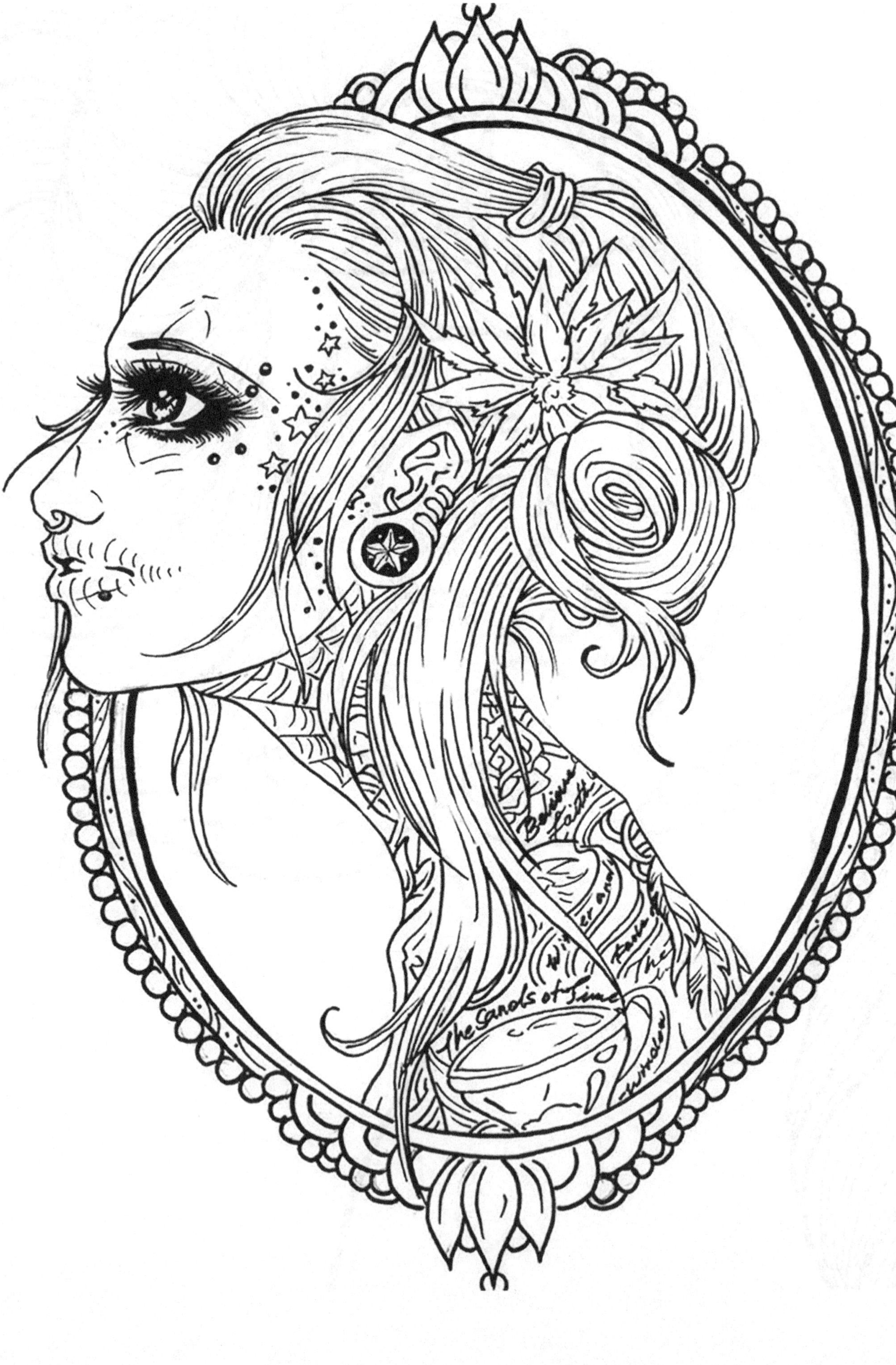
Believe
Faith
The Sands of Time

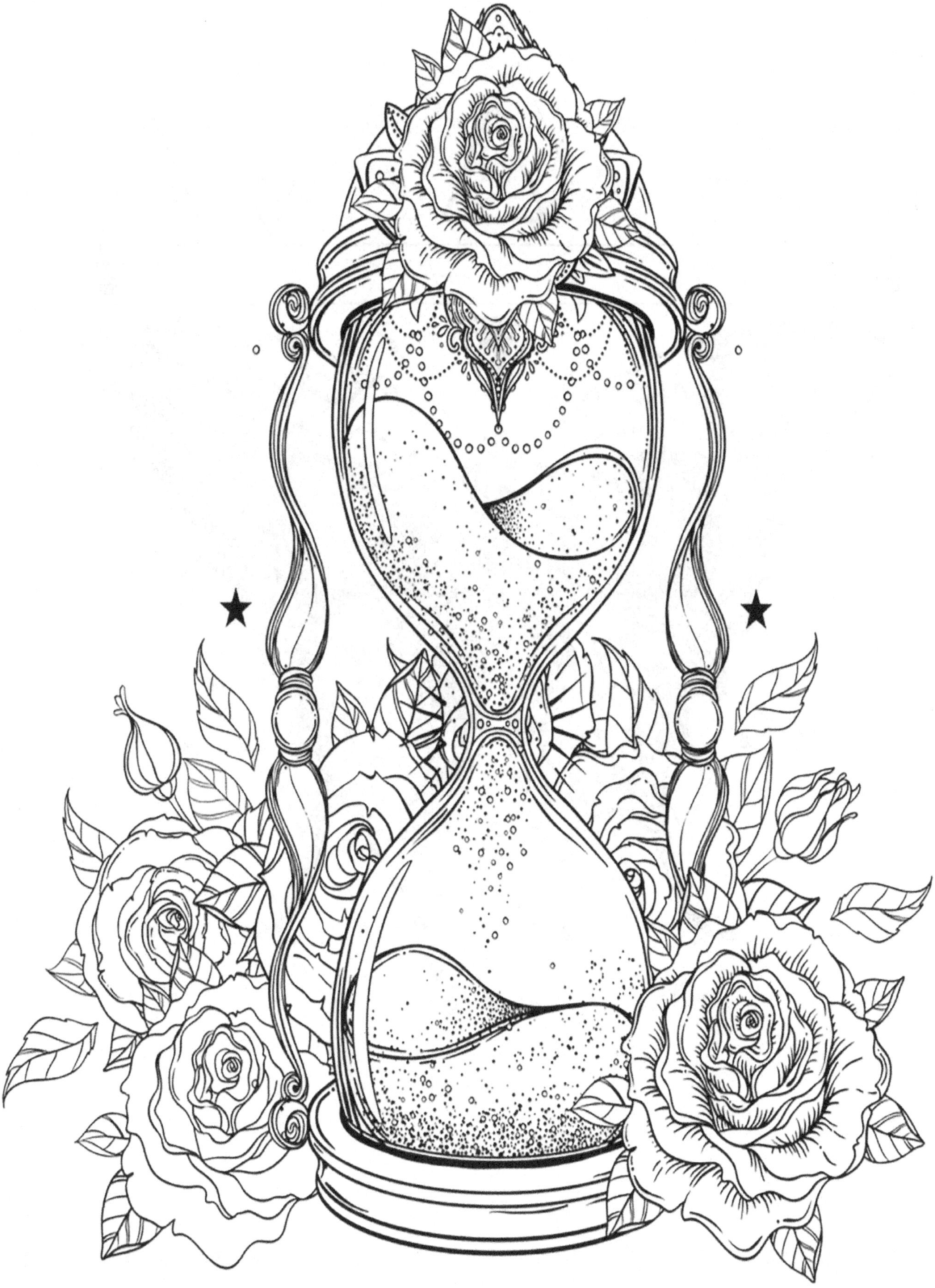

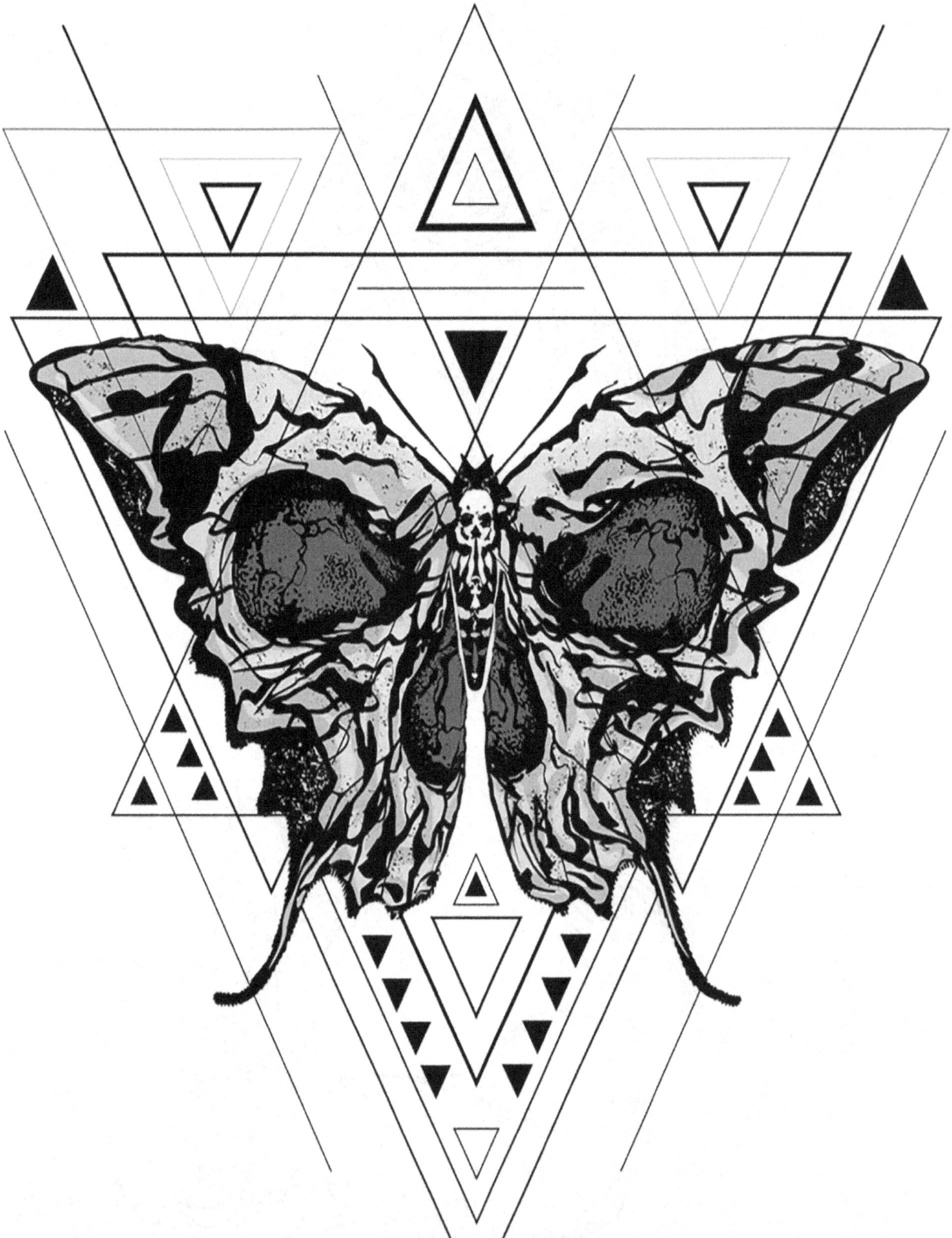

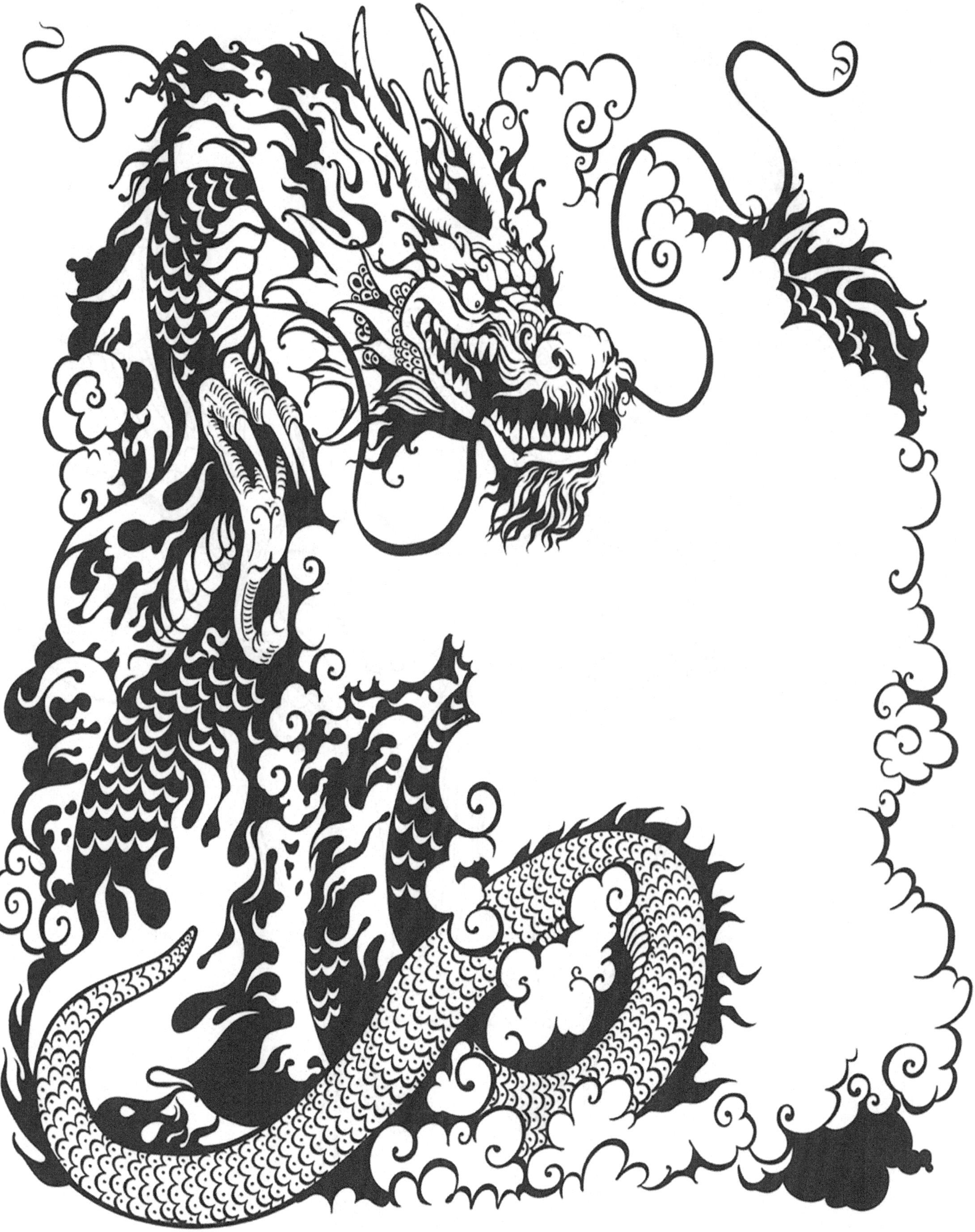

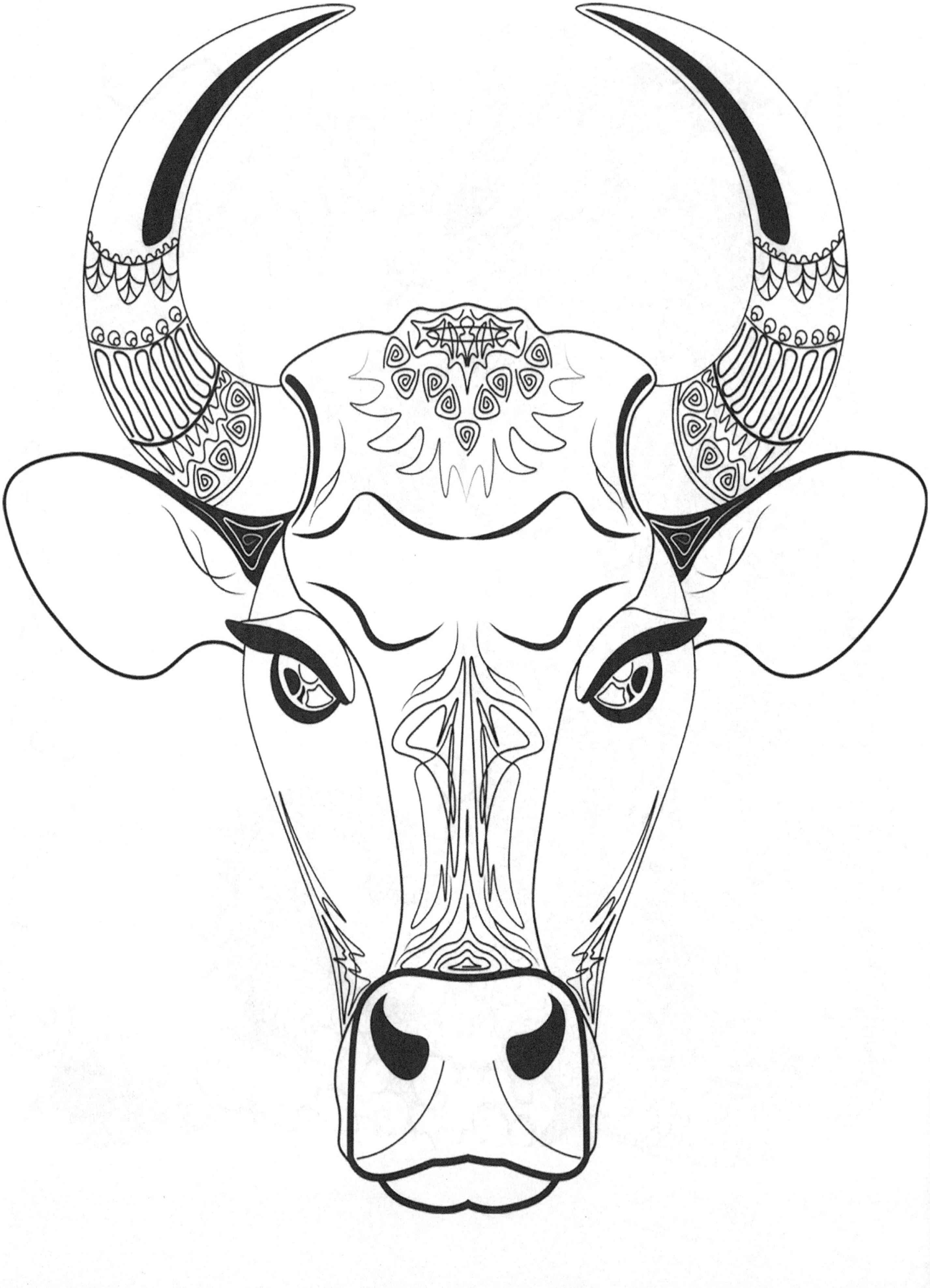

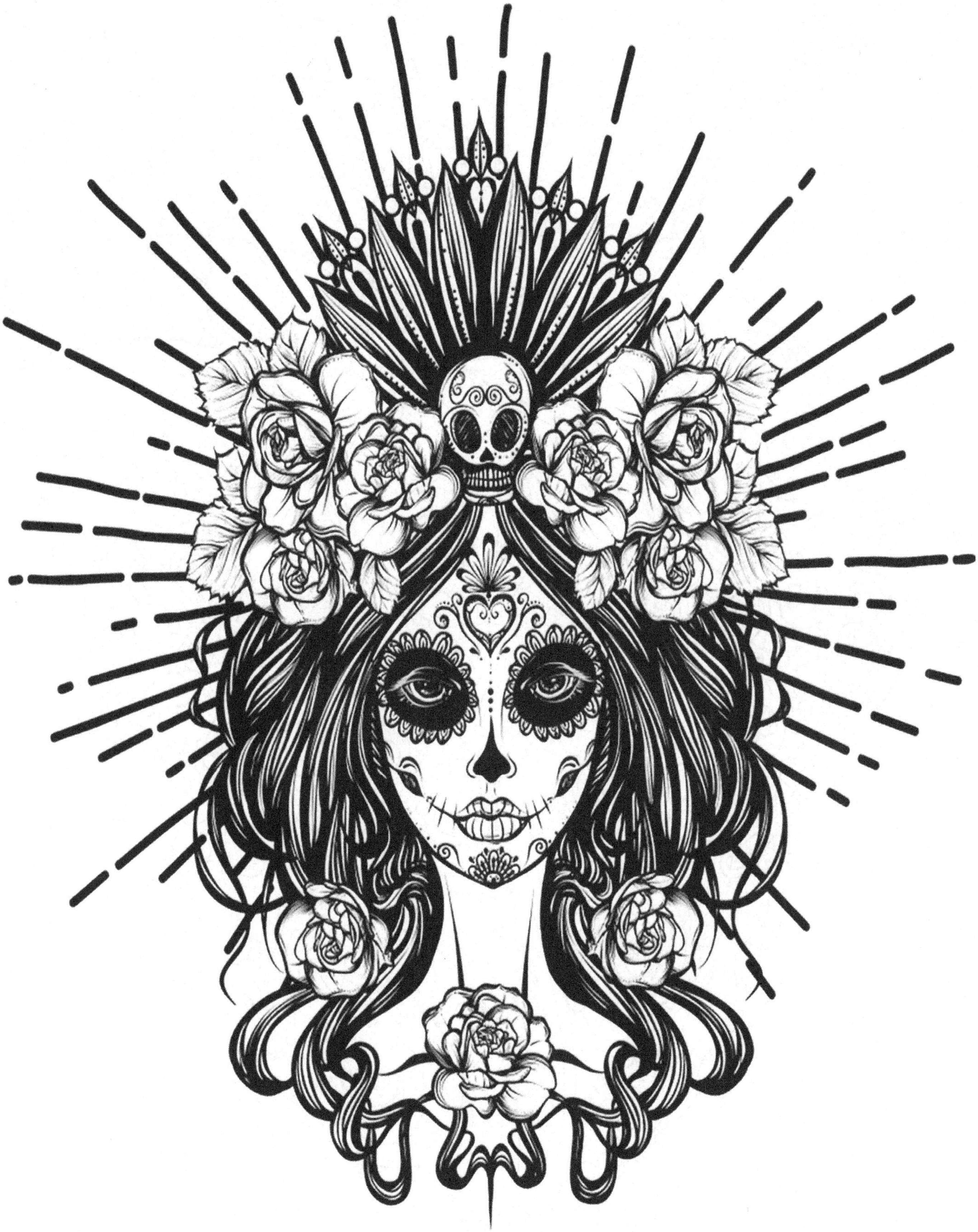

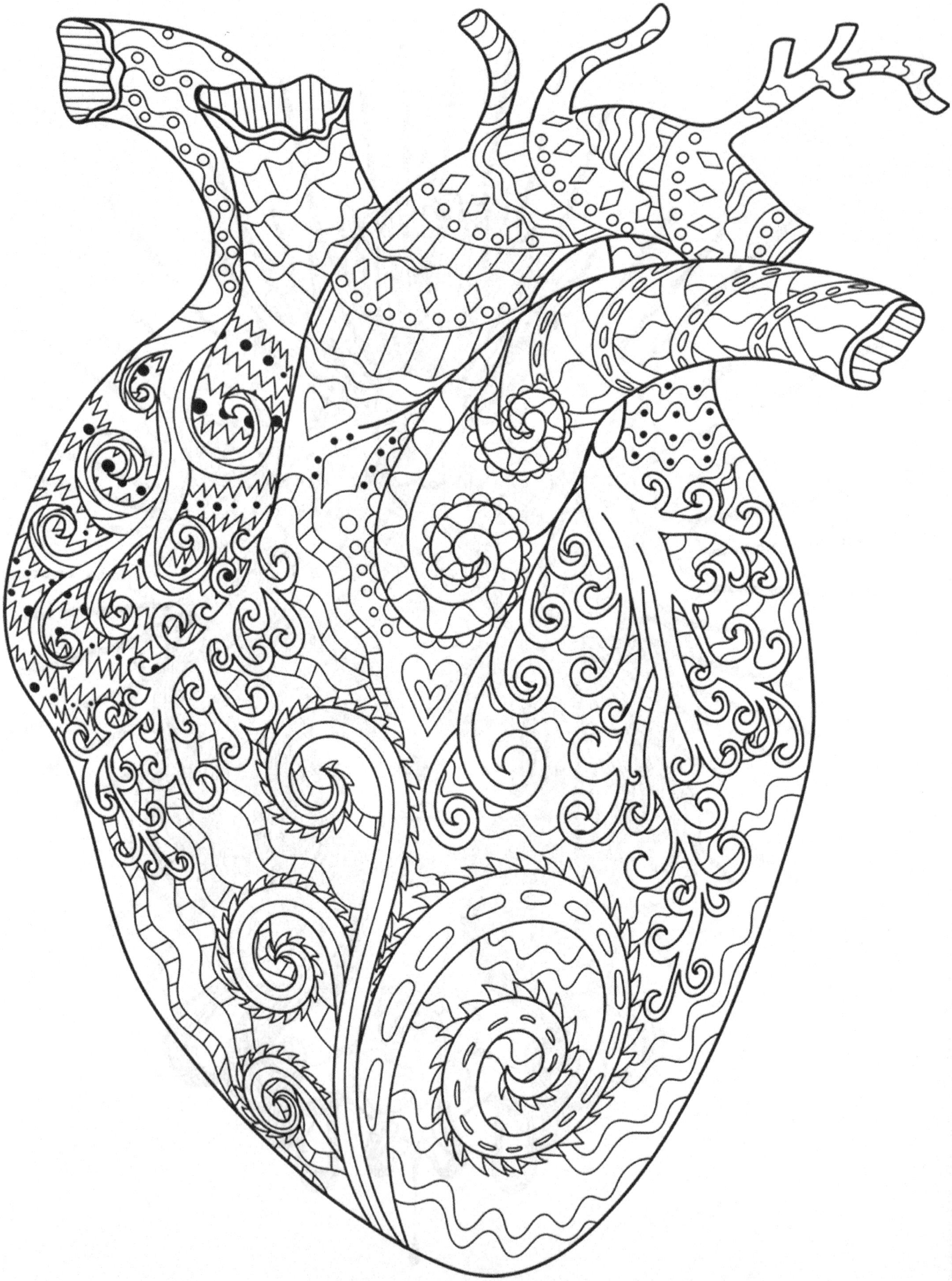

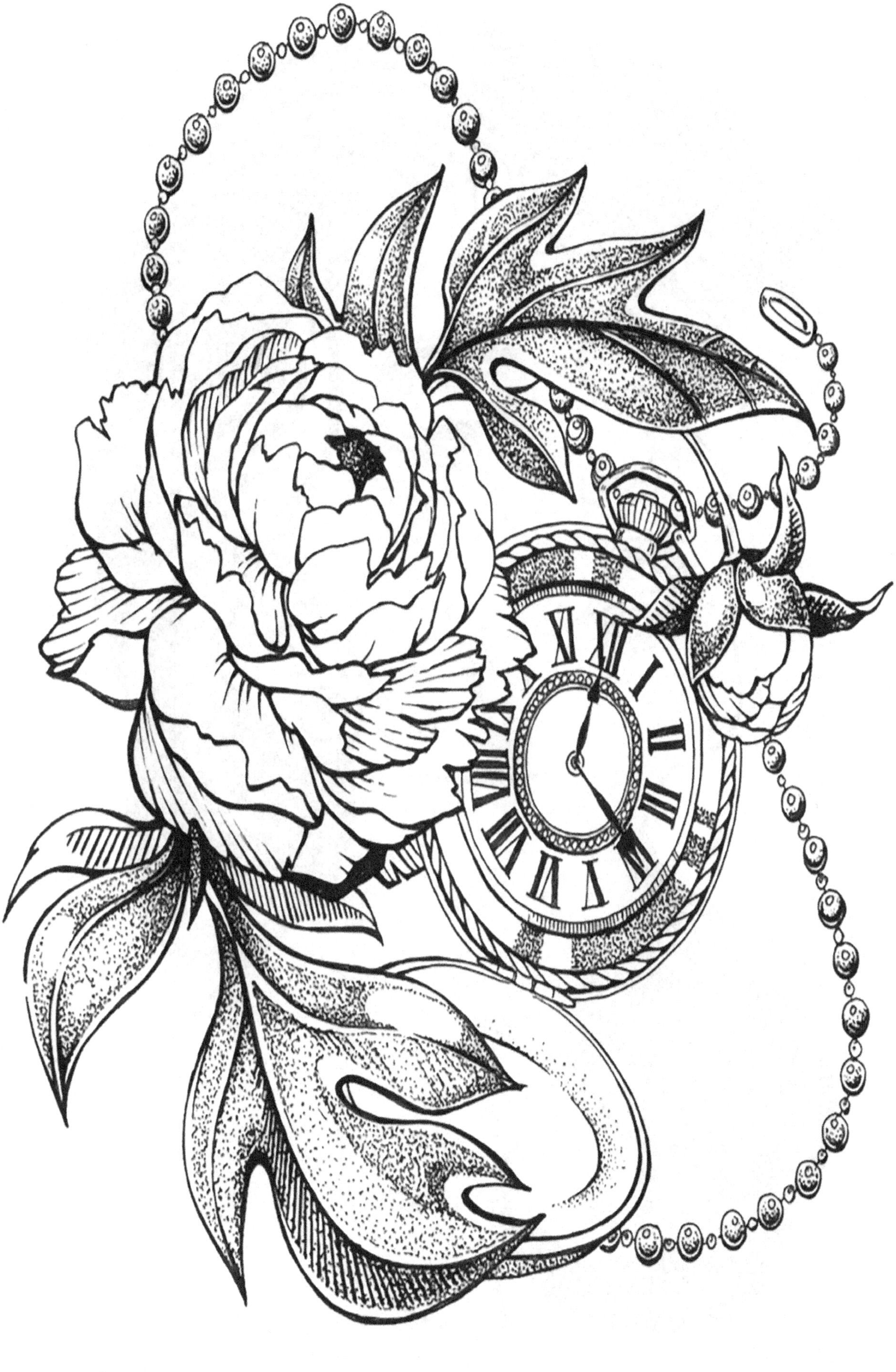

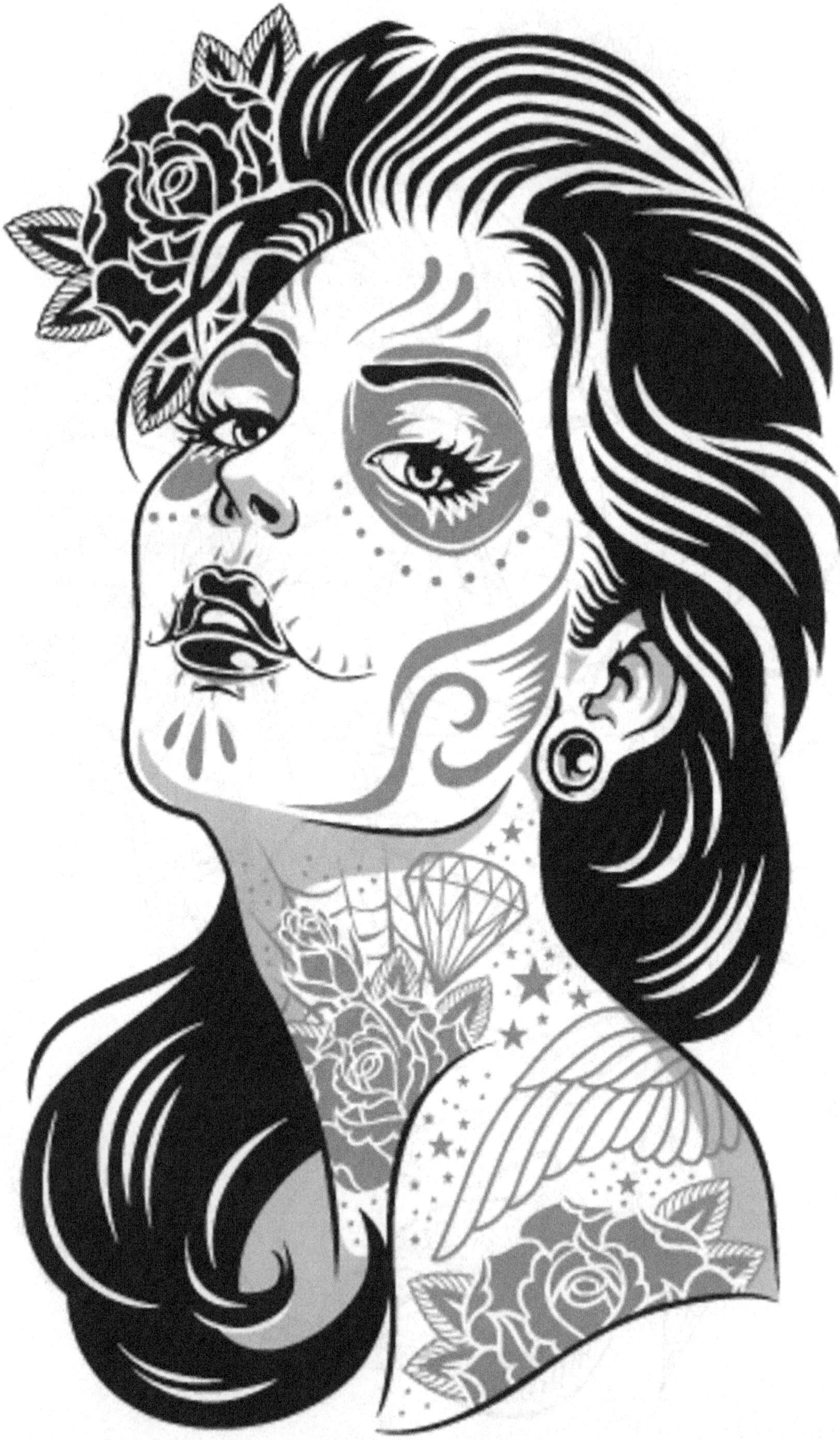

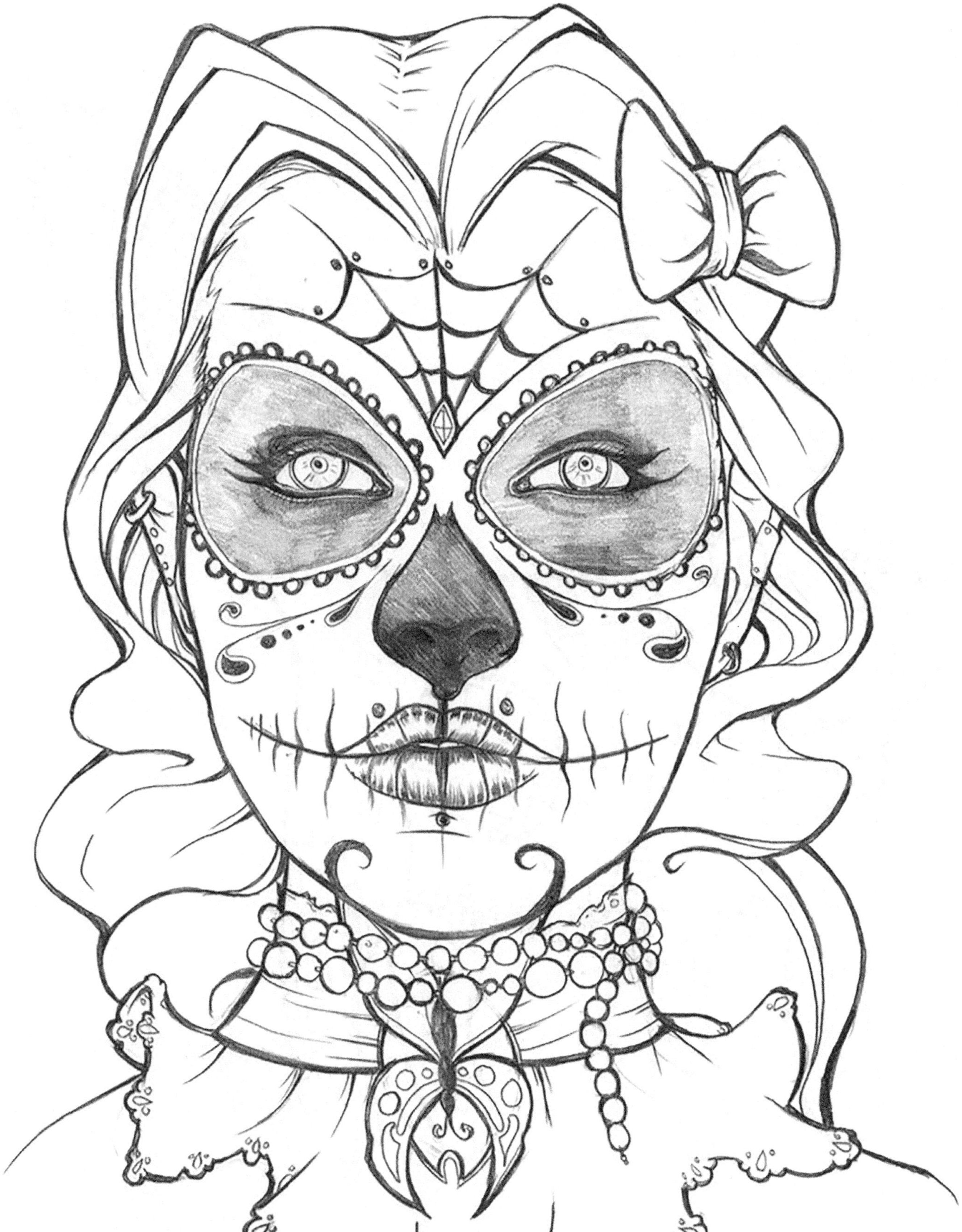

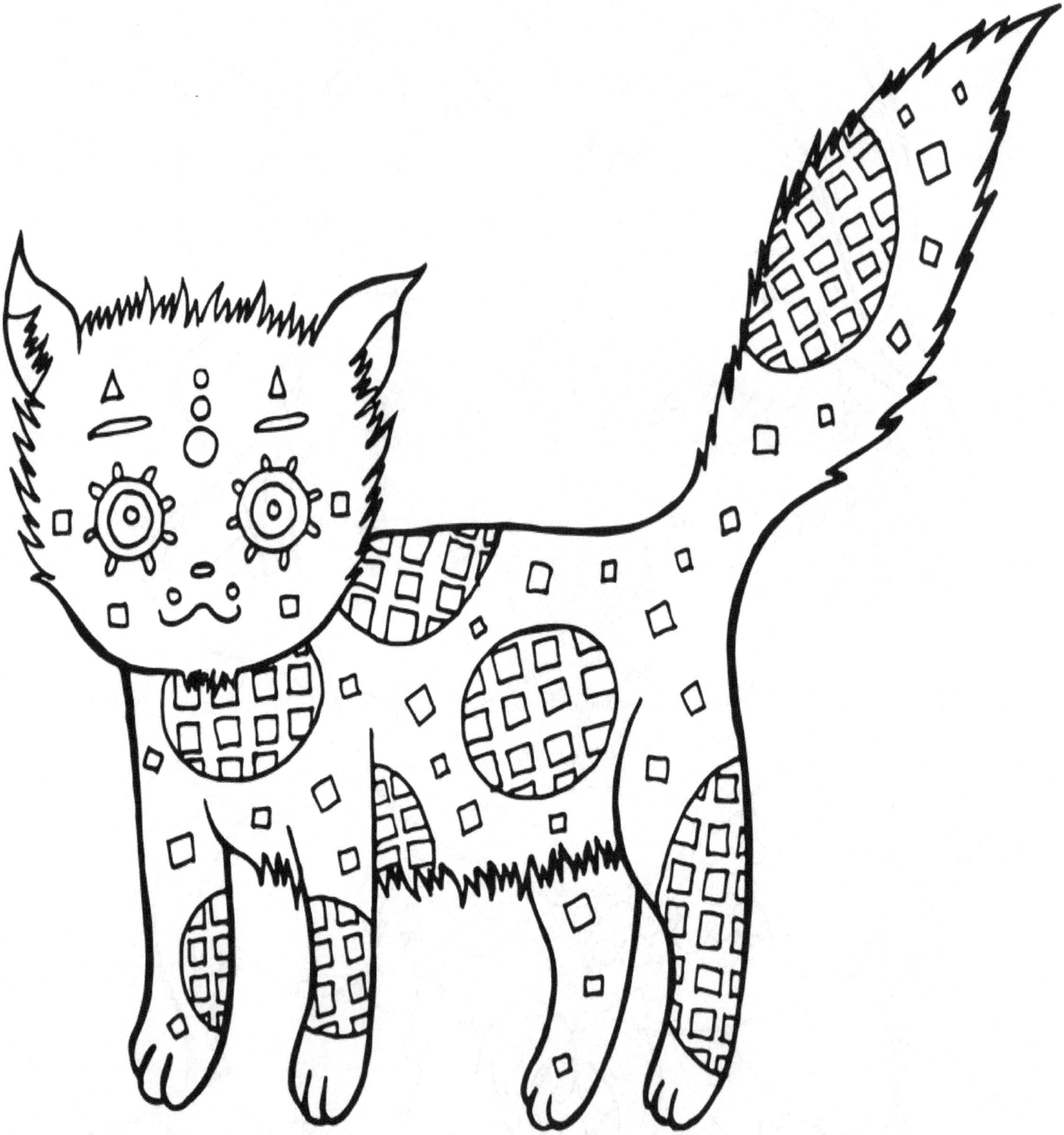

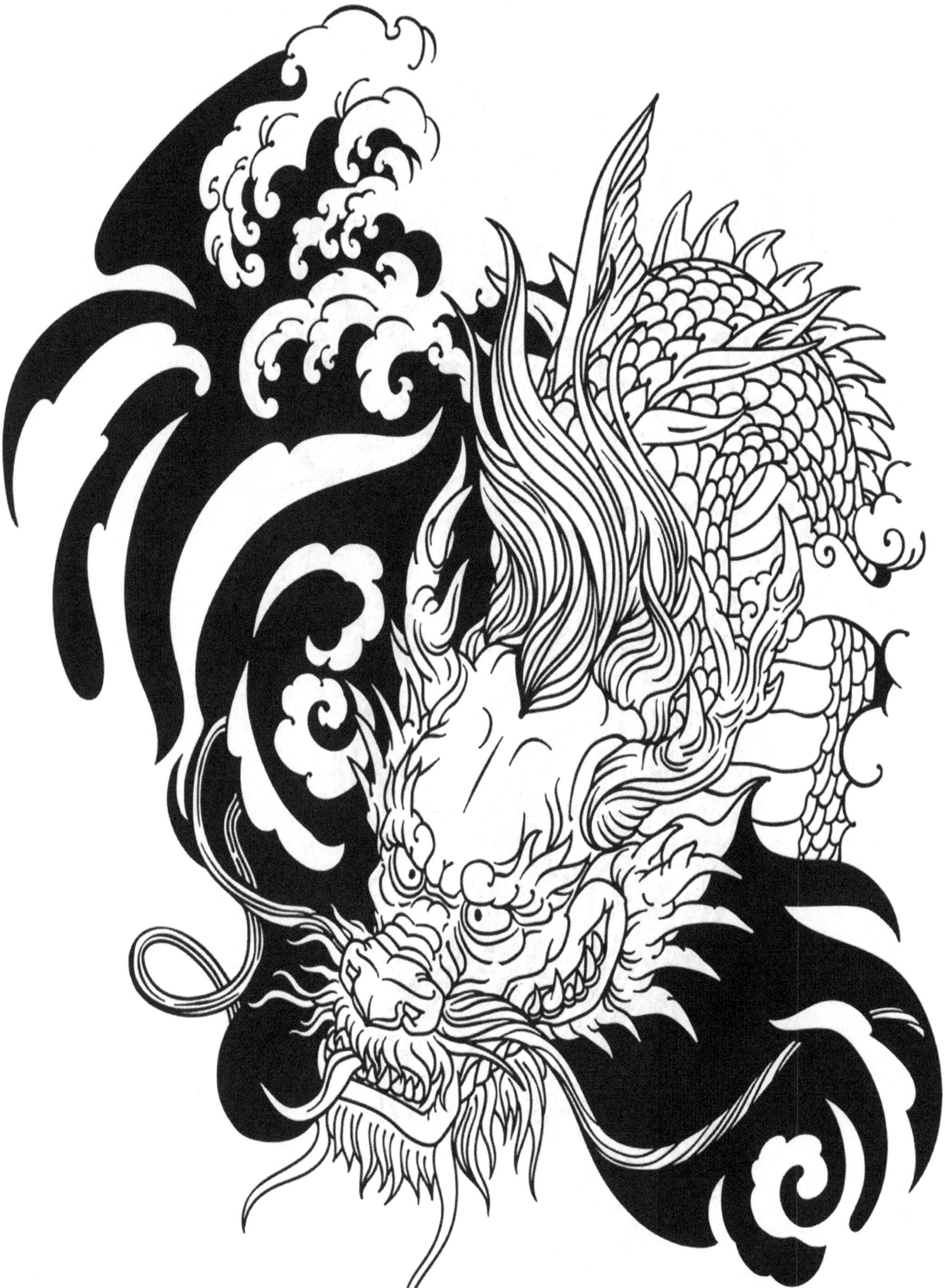

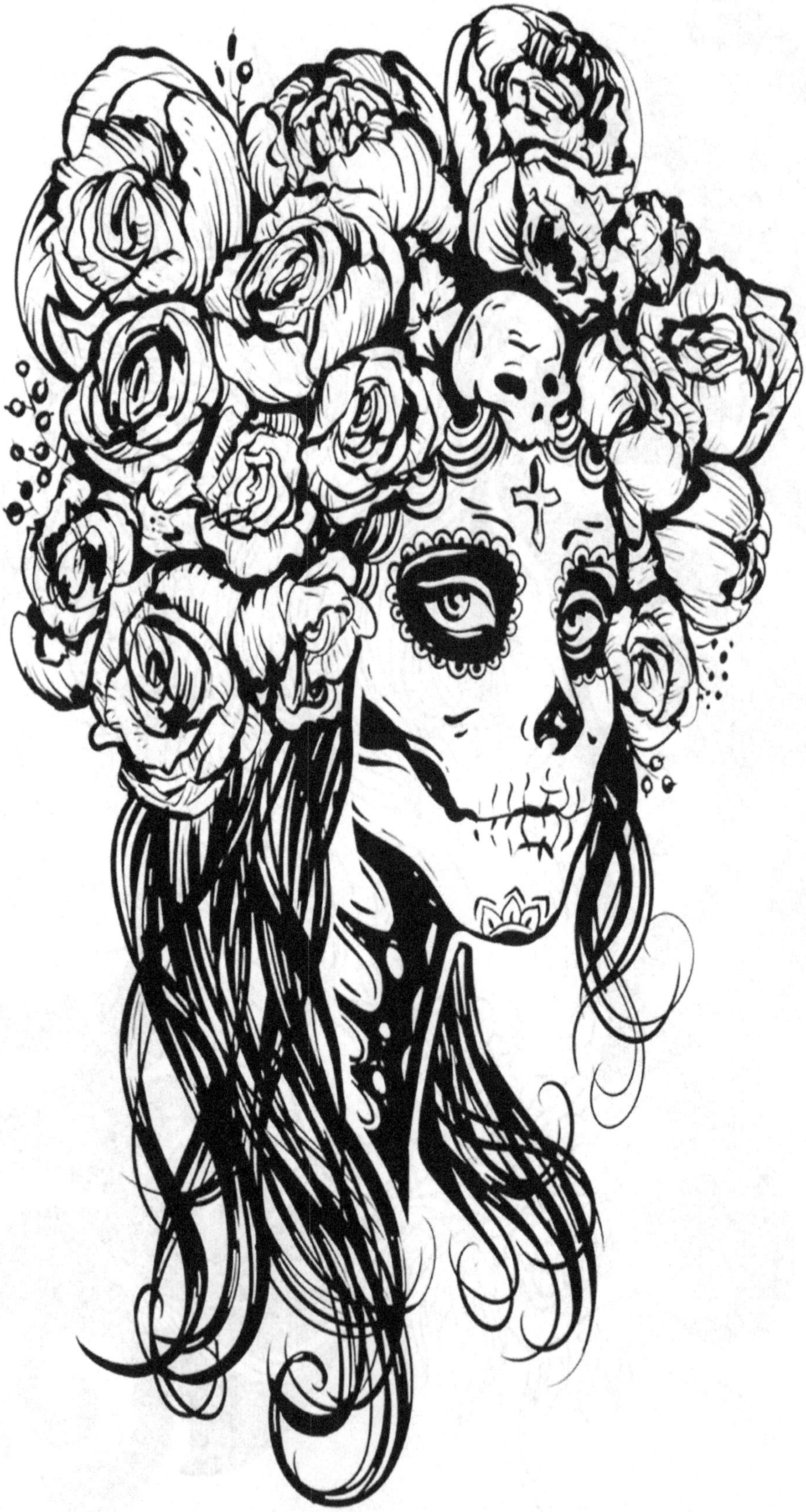

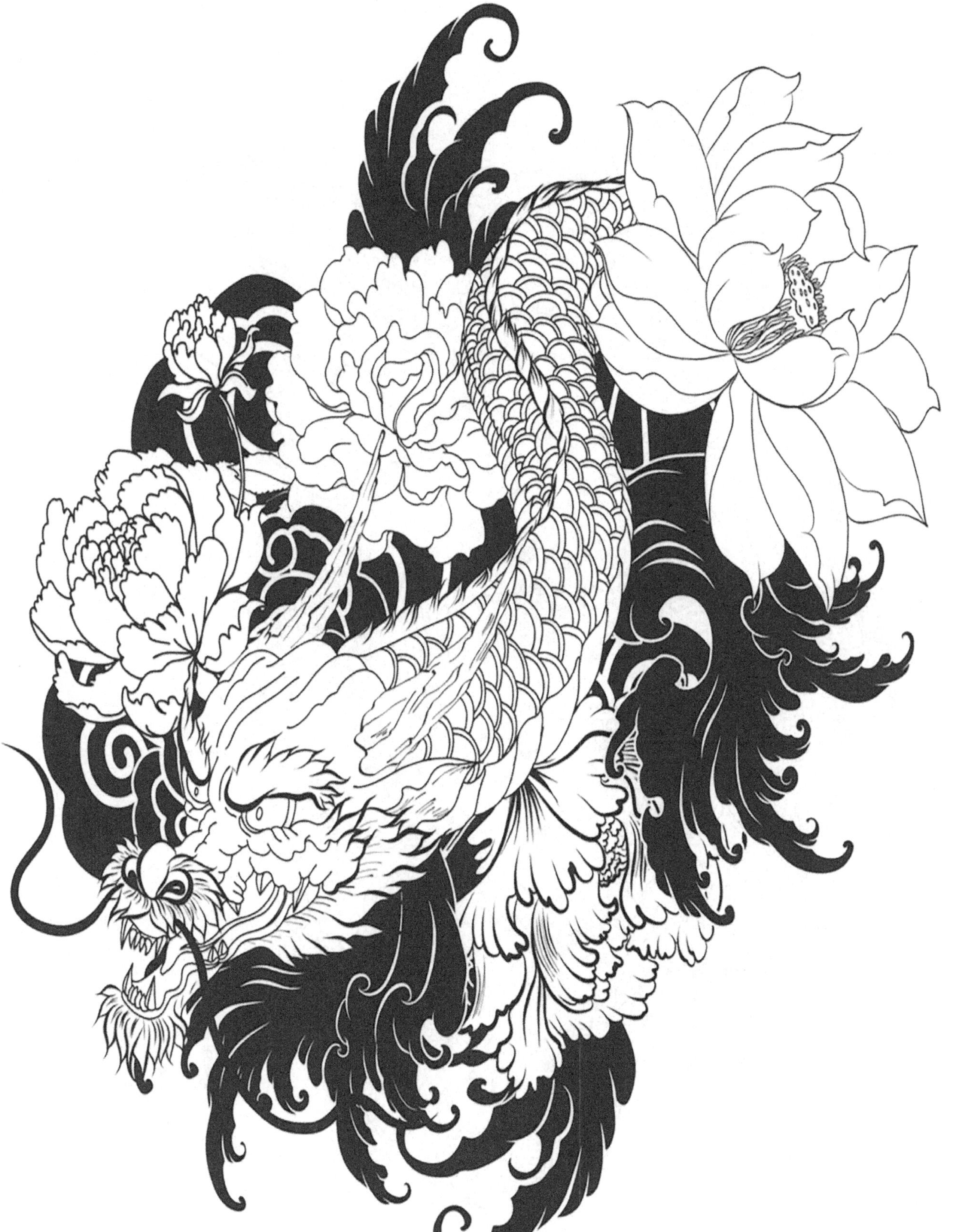

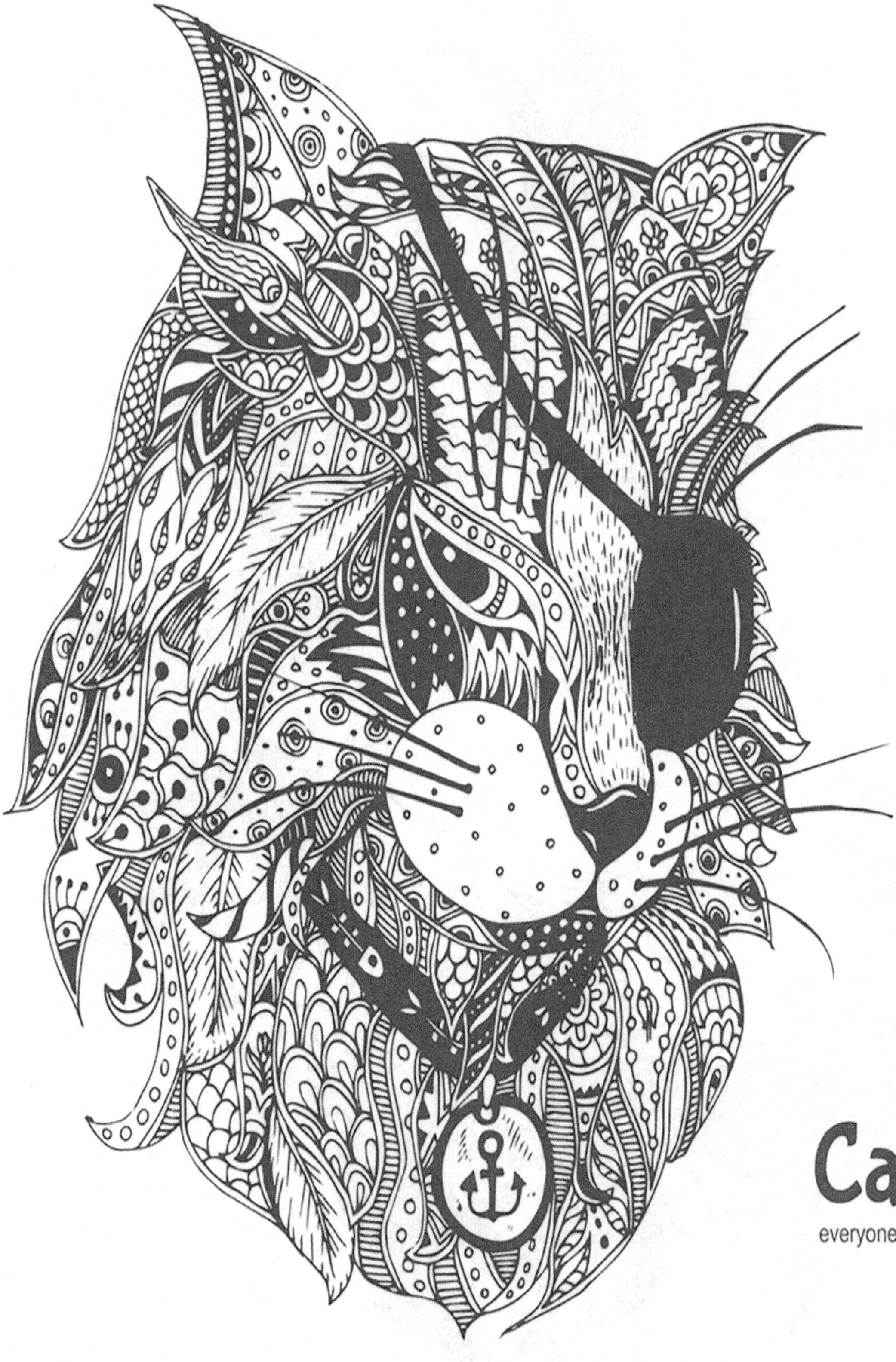

Cat

everyone loves cats

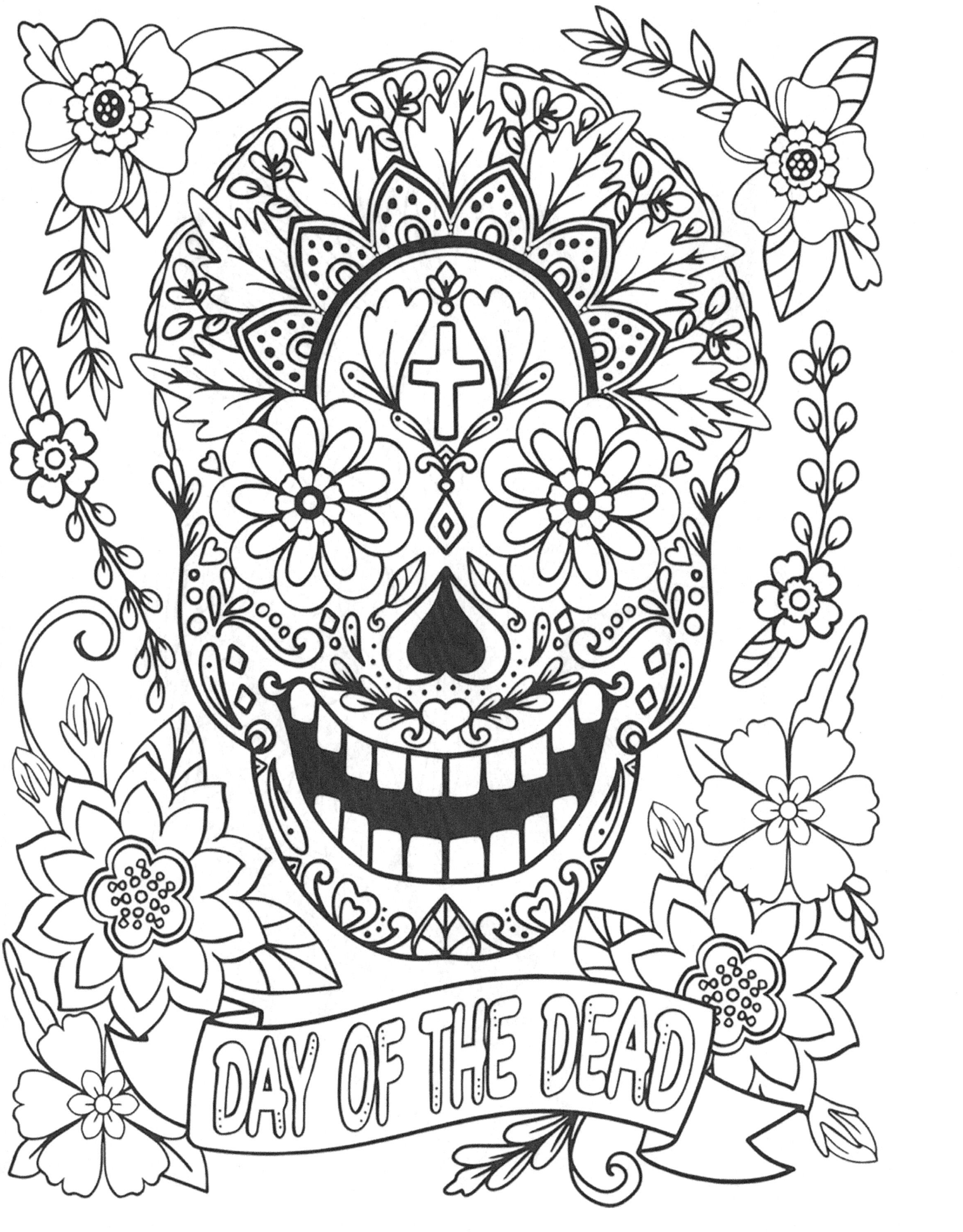
DAY OF THE DEAD

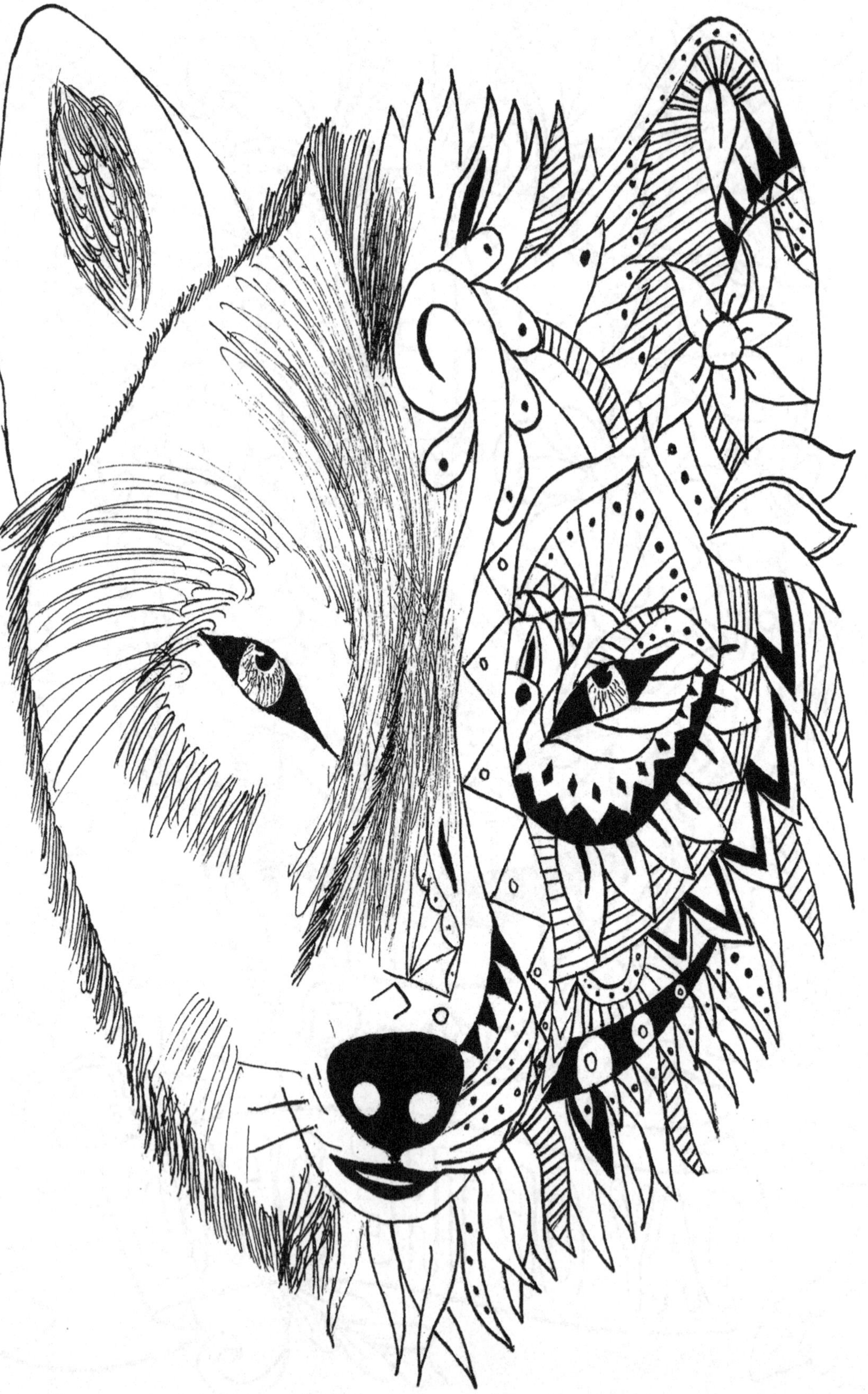

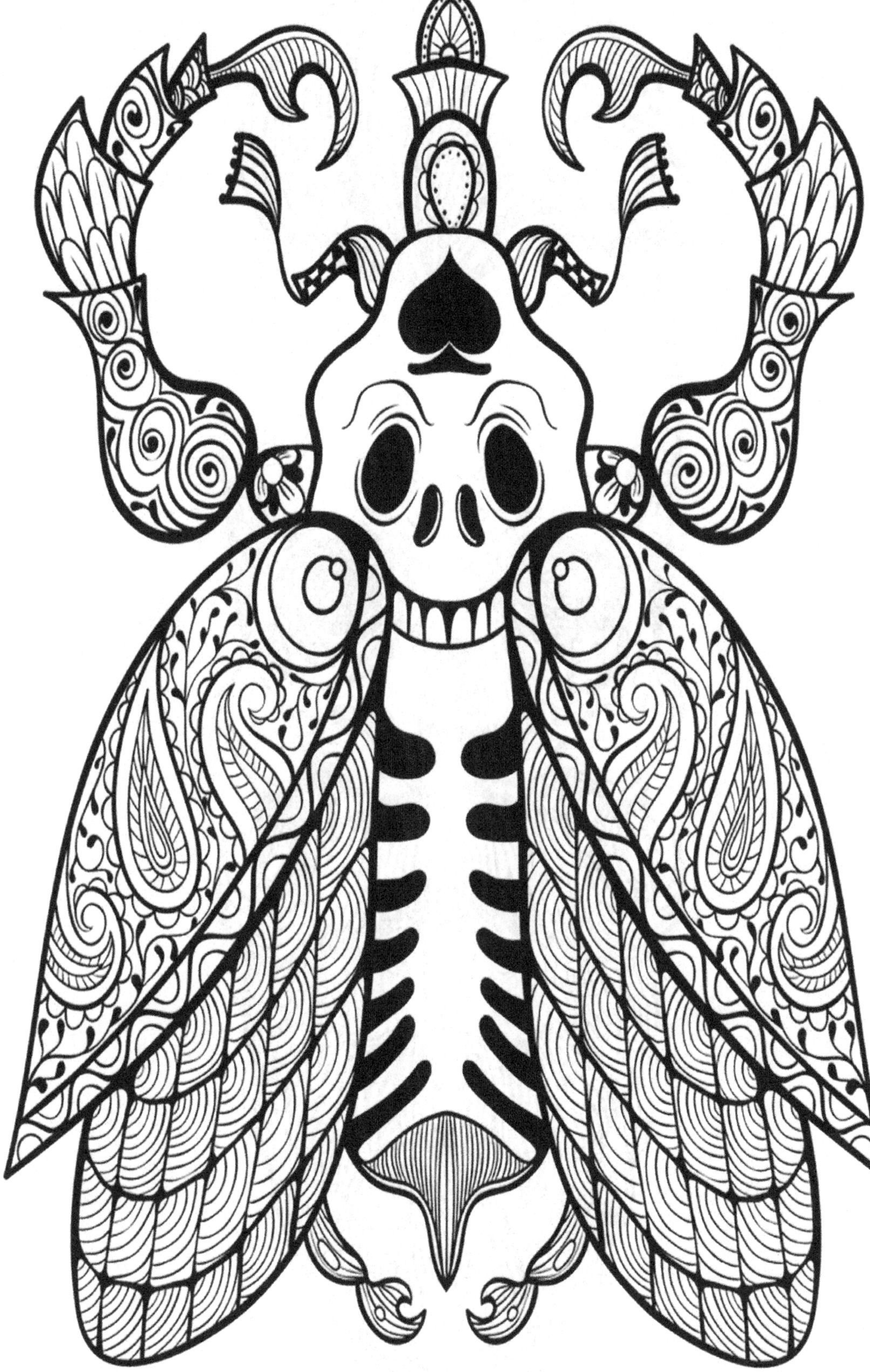

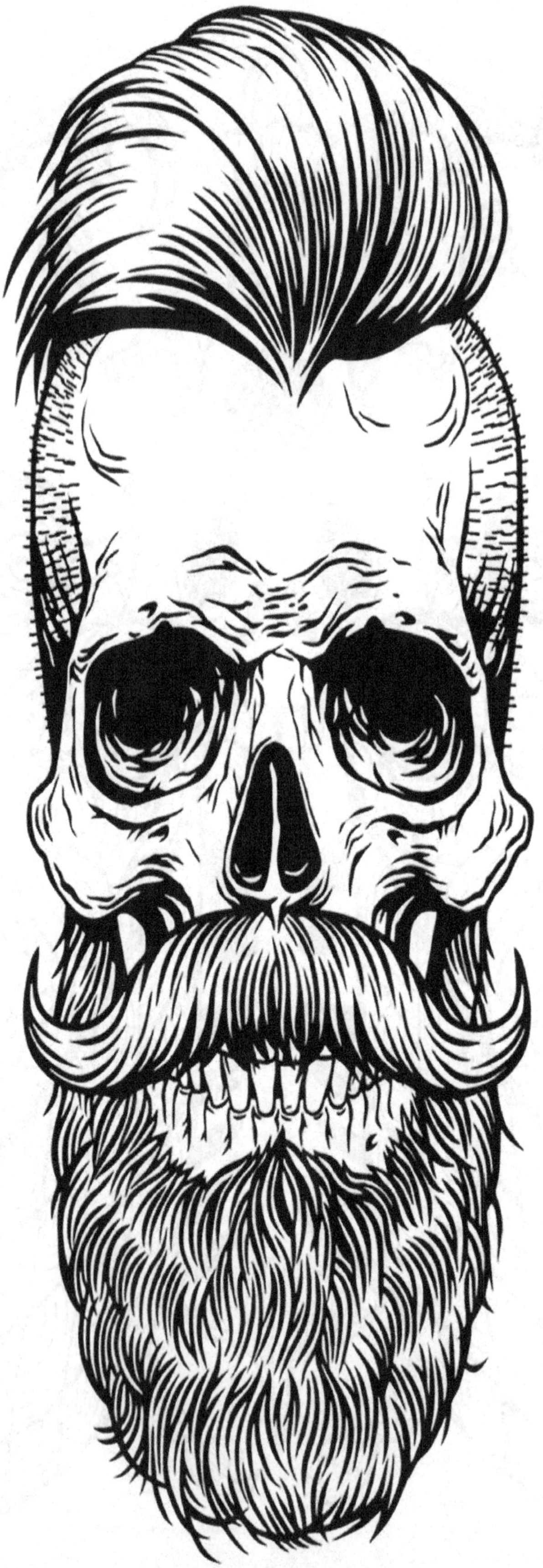

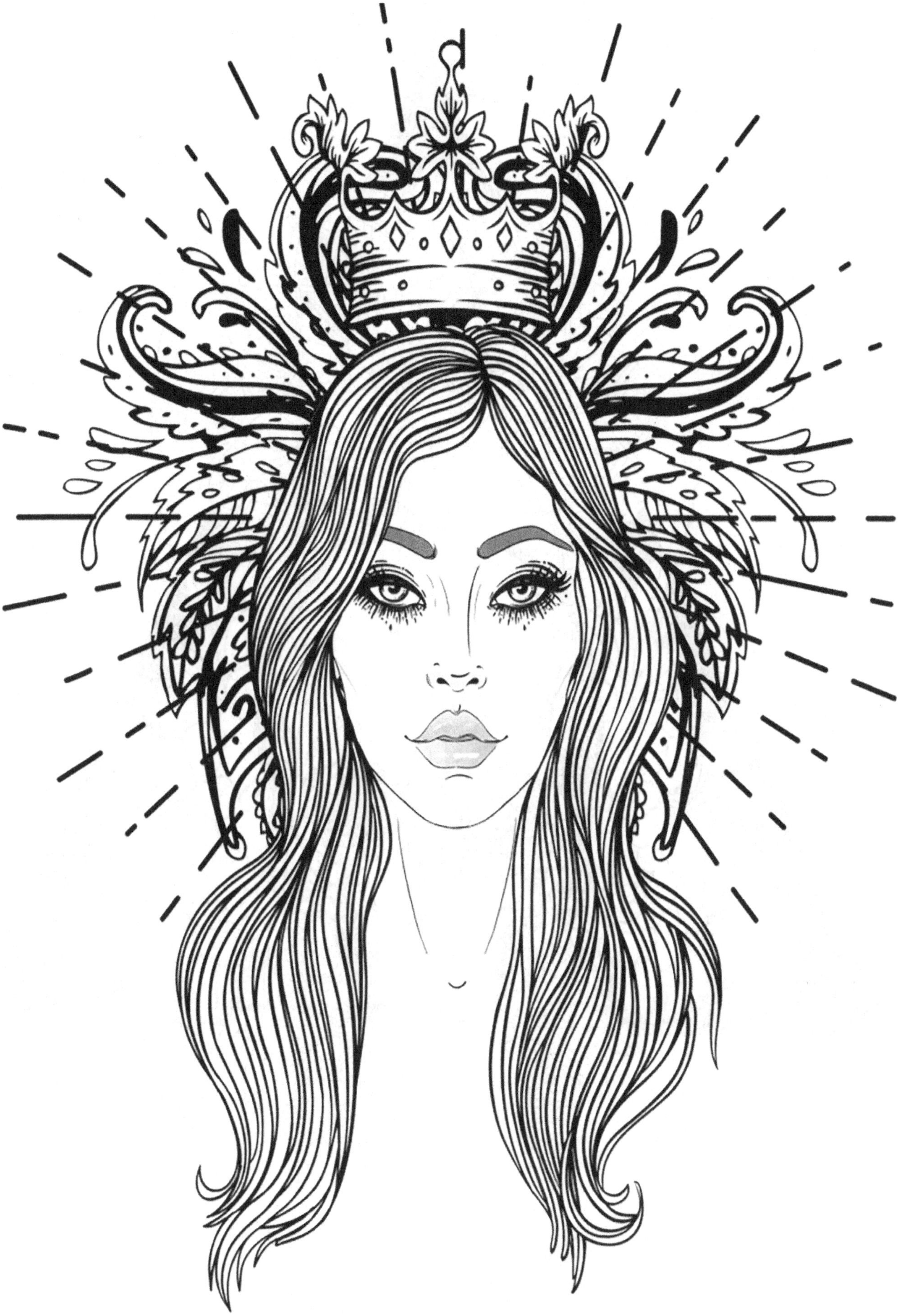

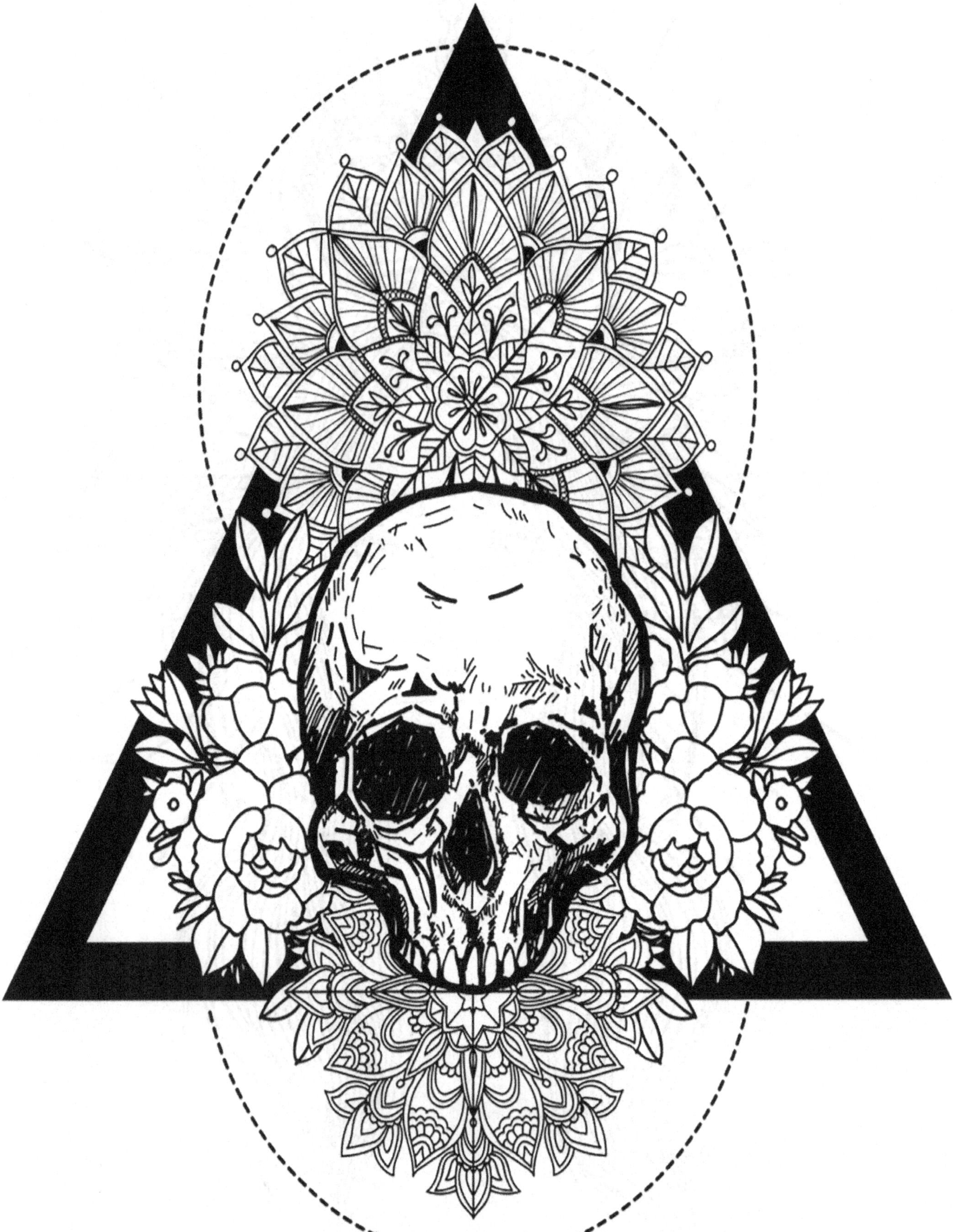

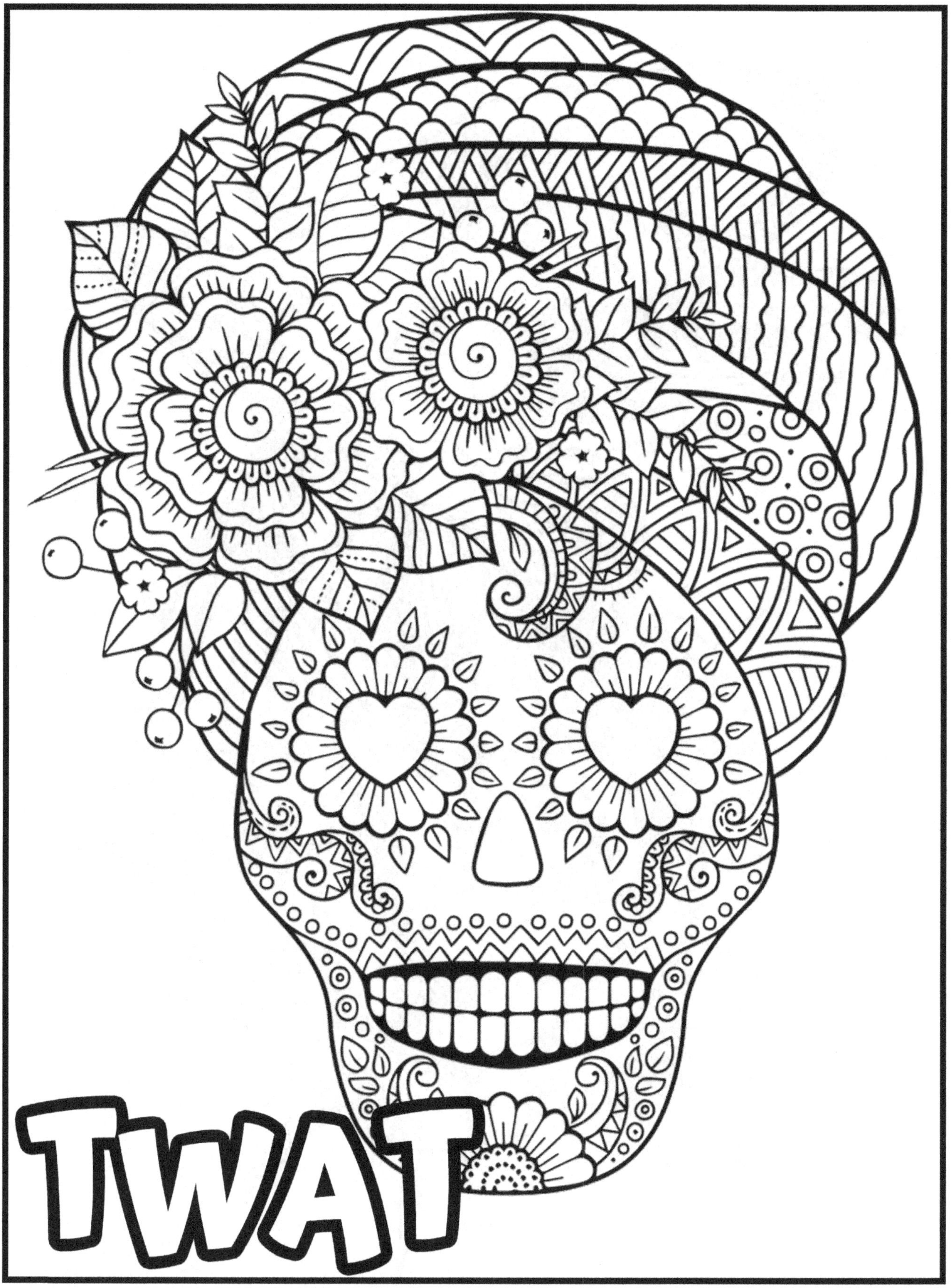
TWAT

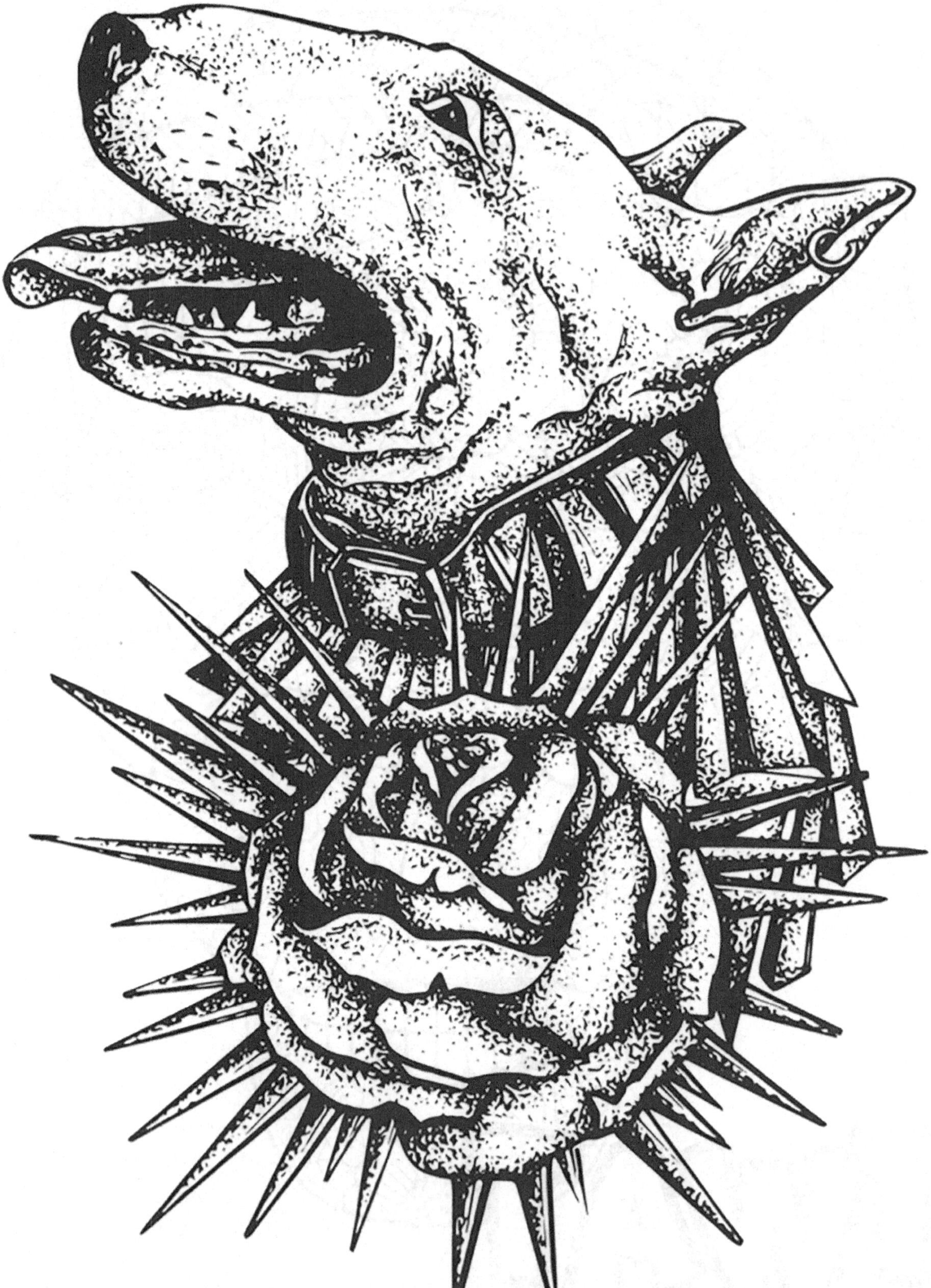

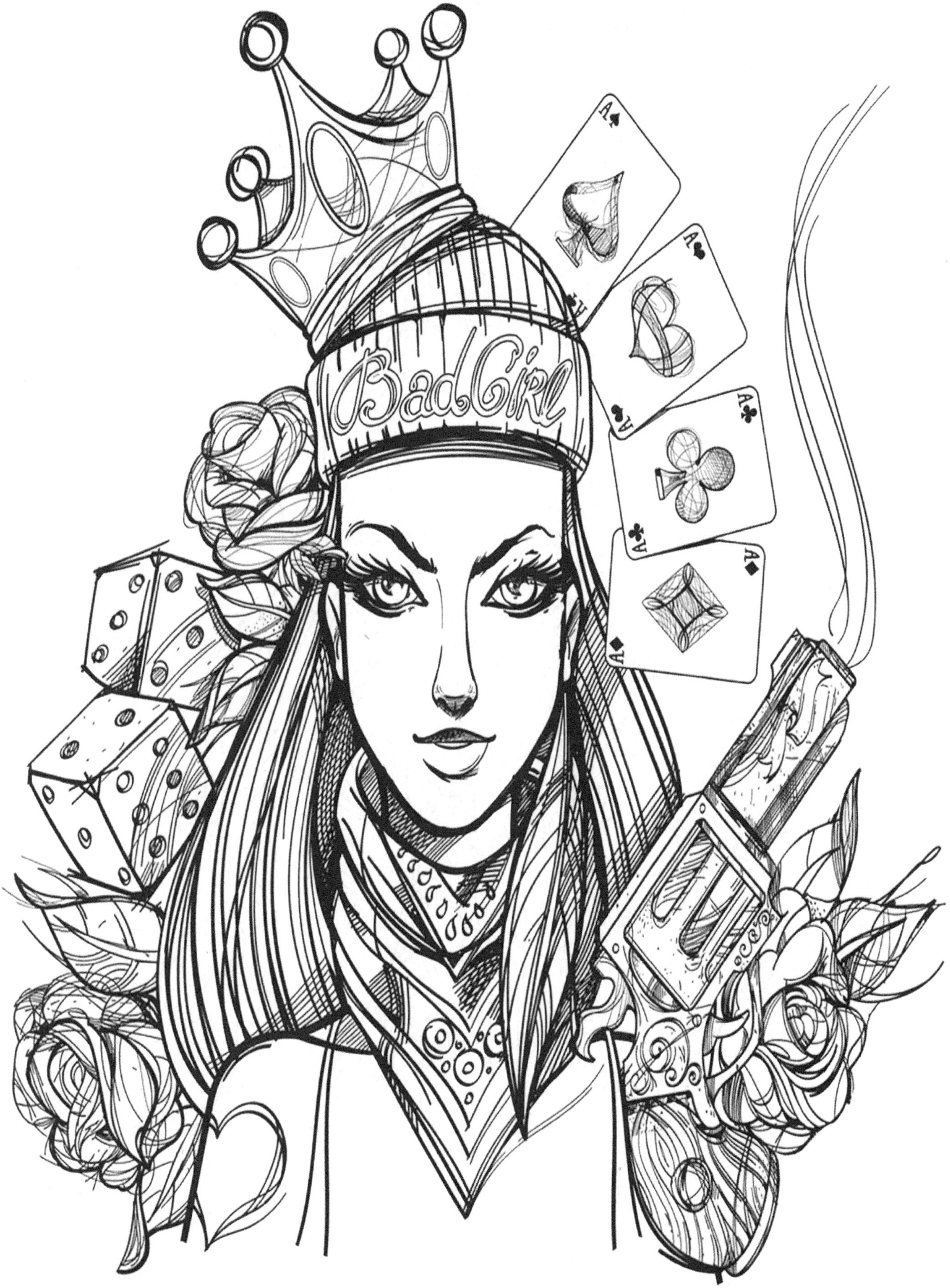
Bad Girl

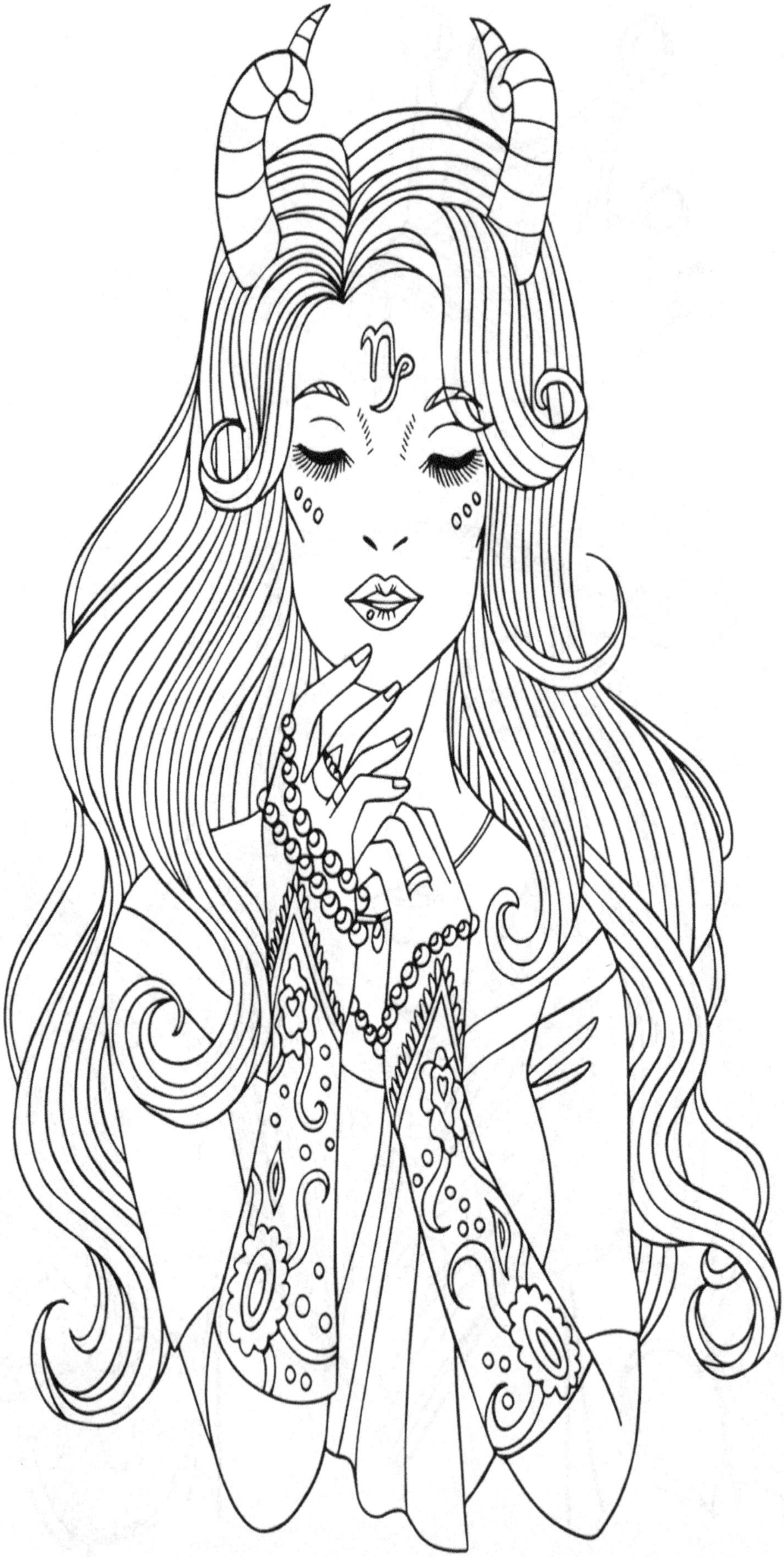

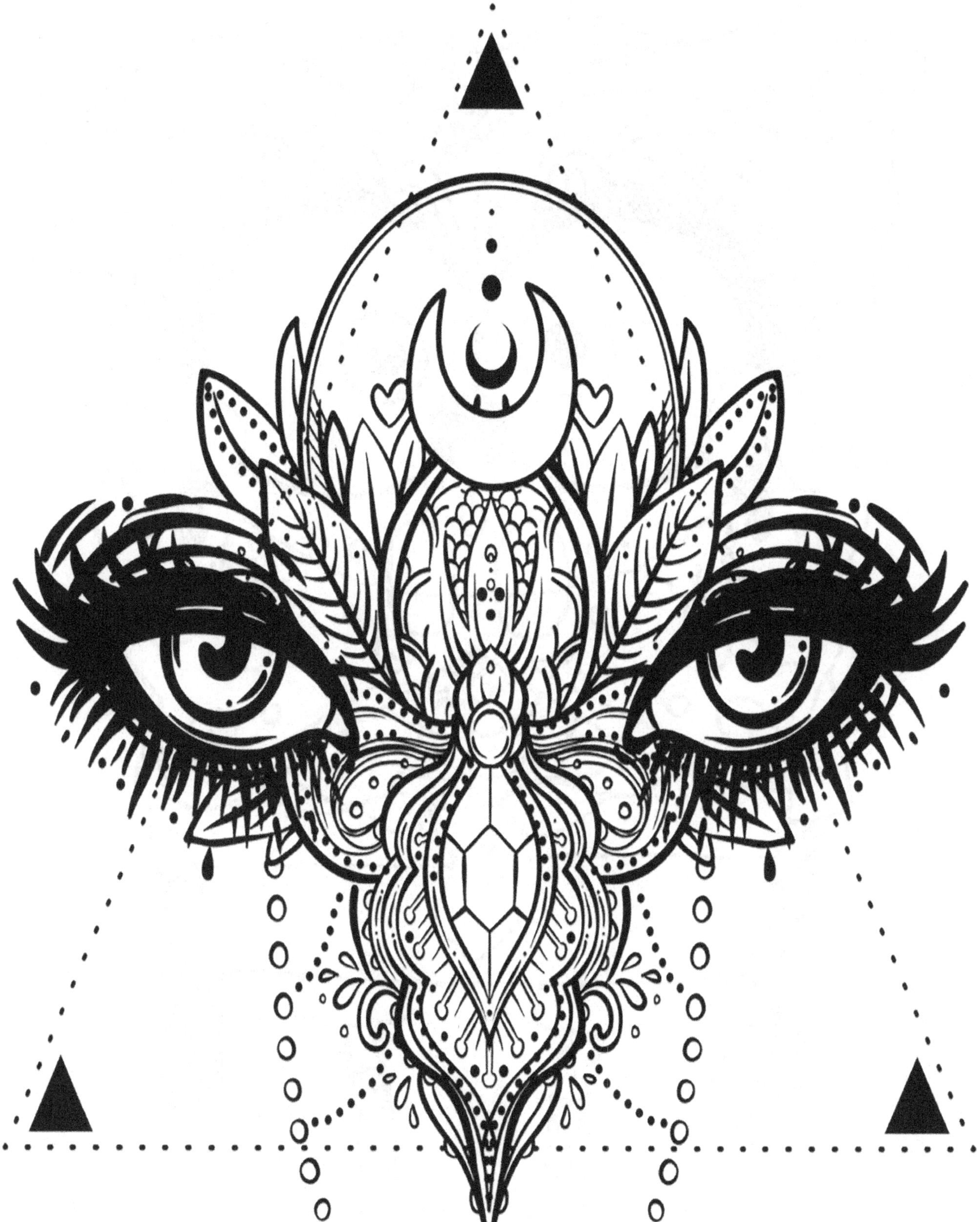

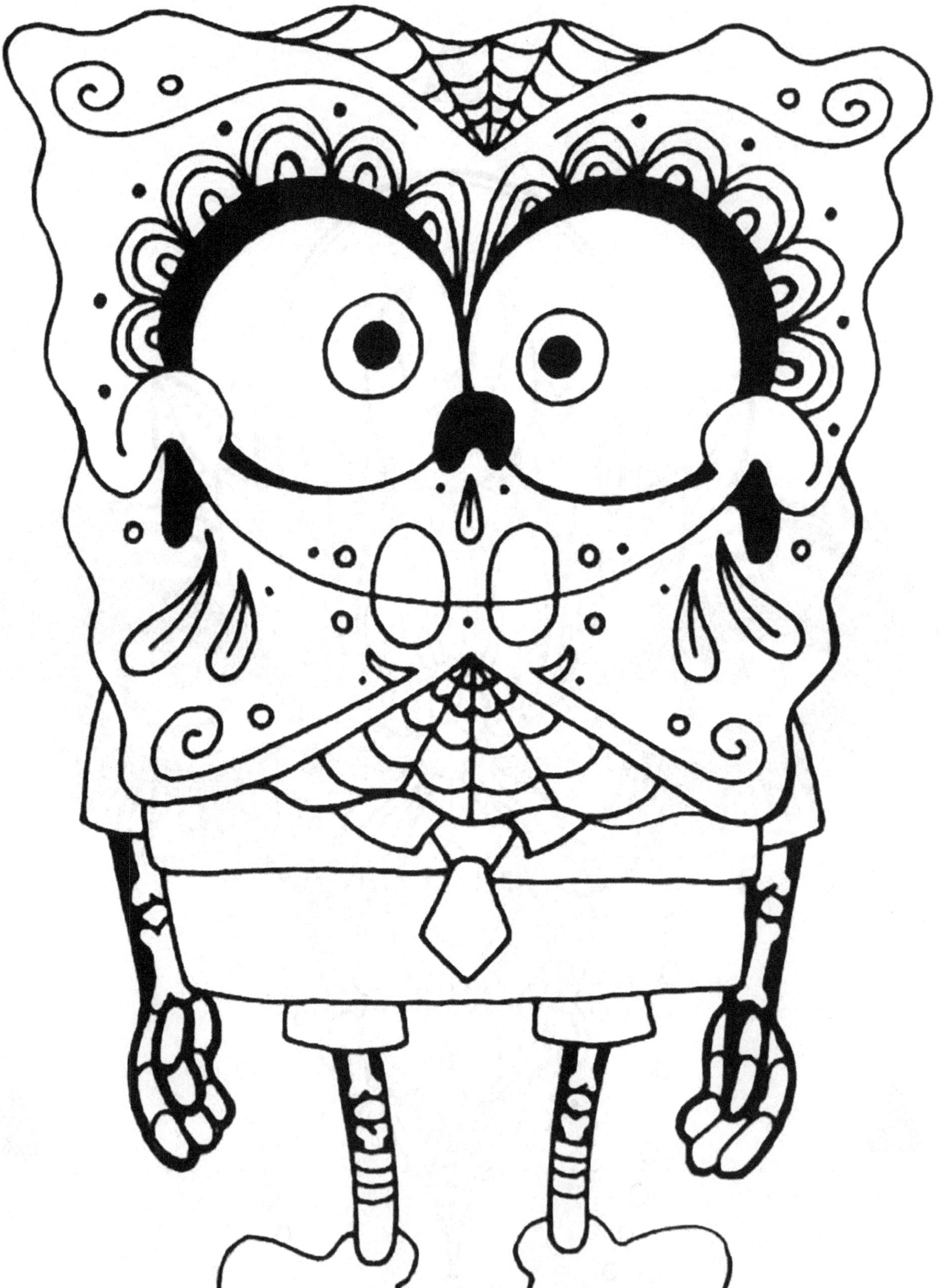

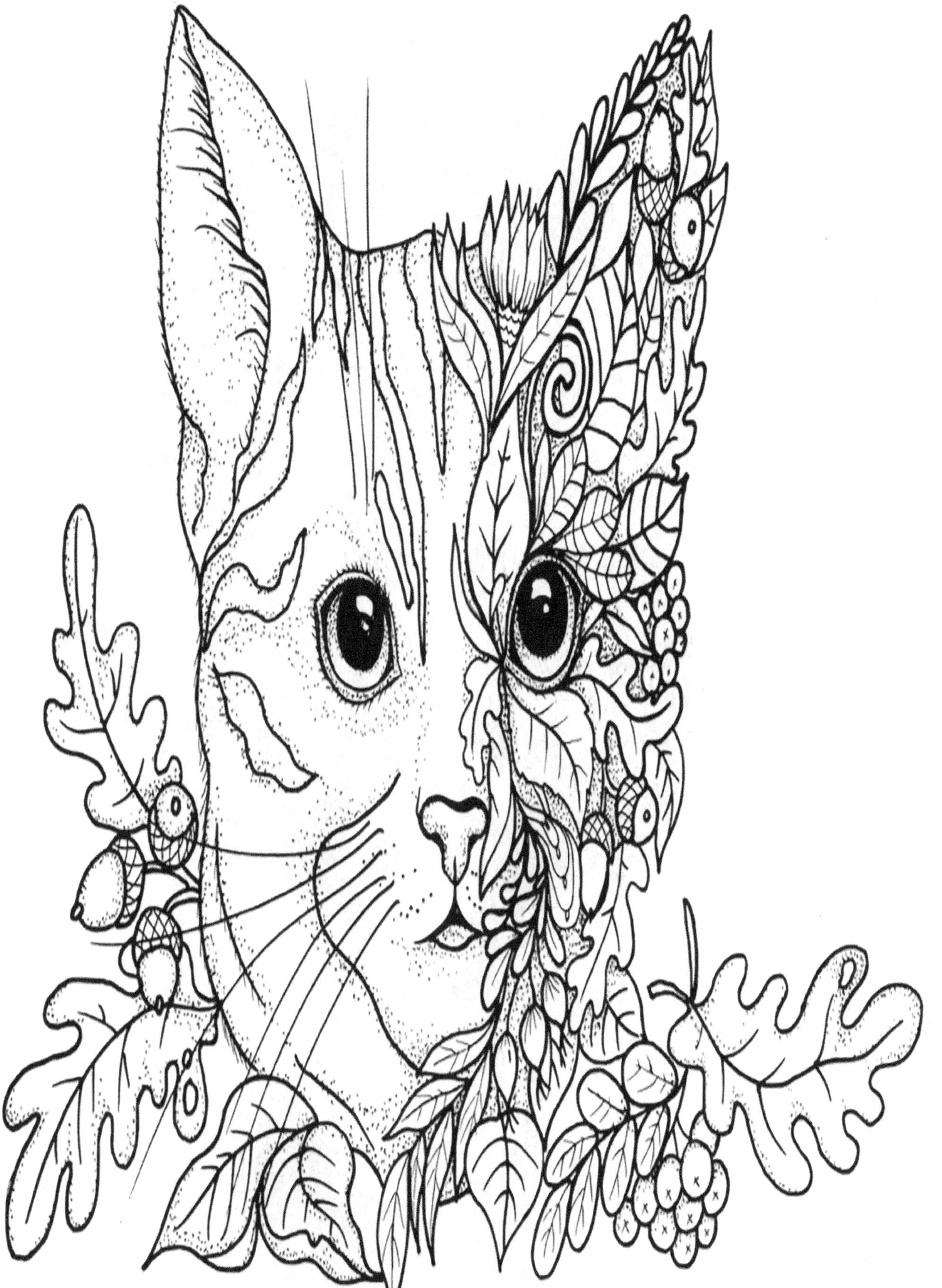

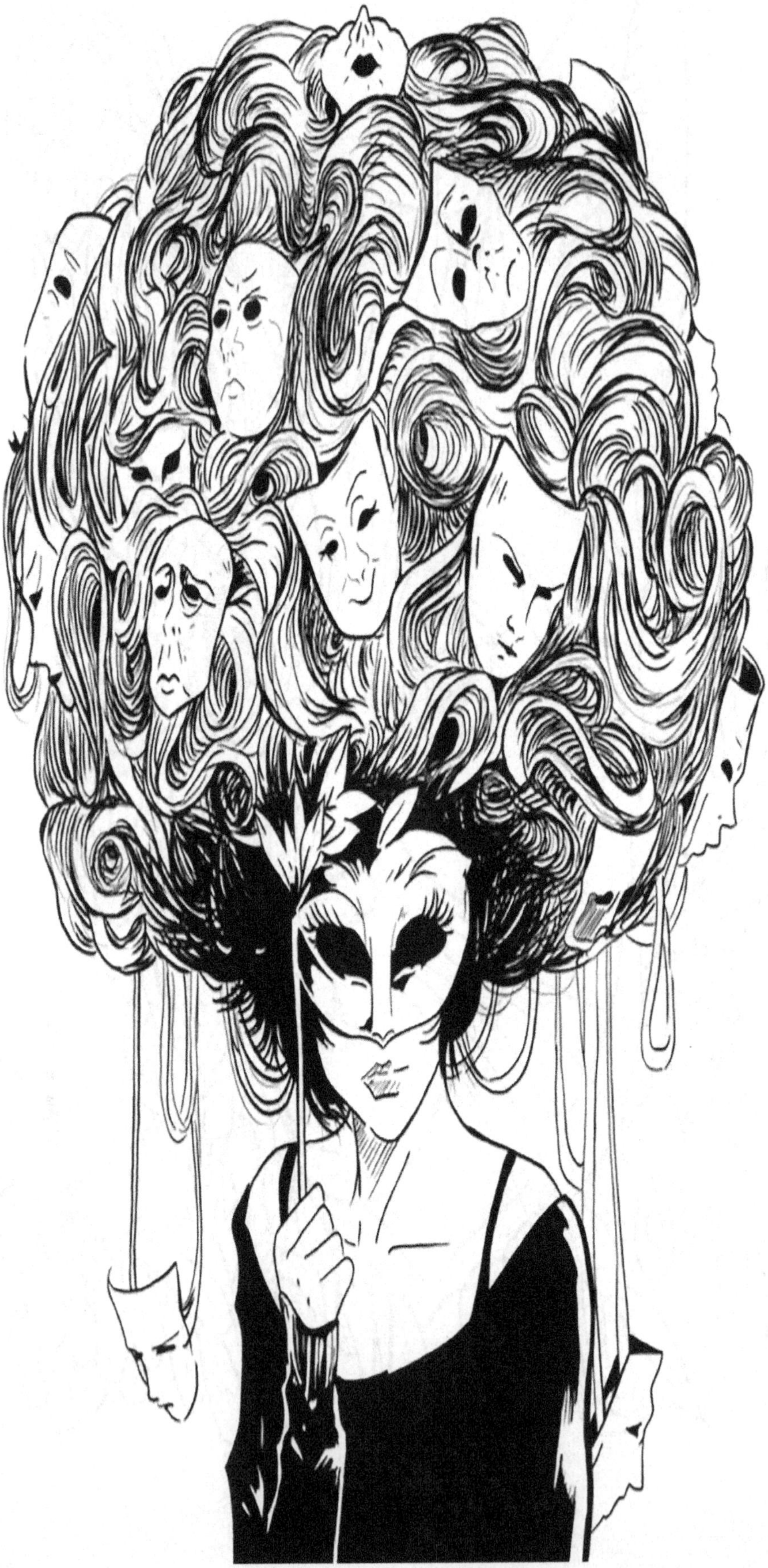

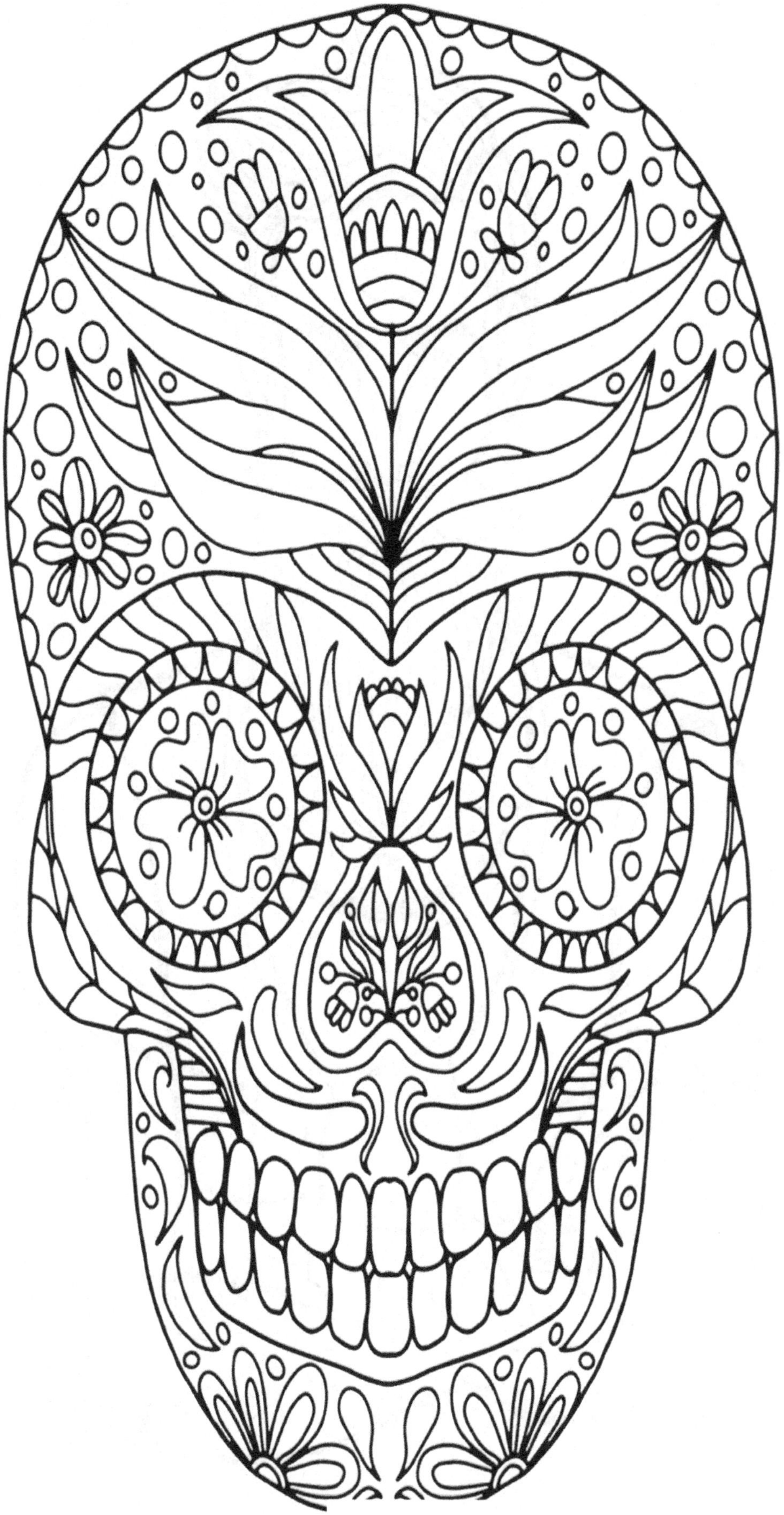

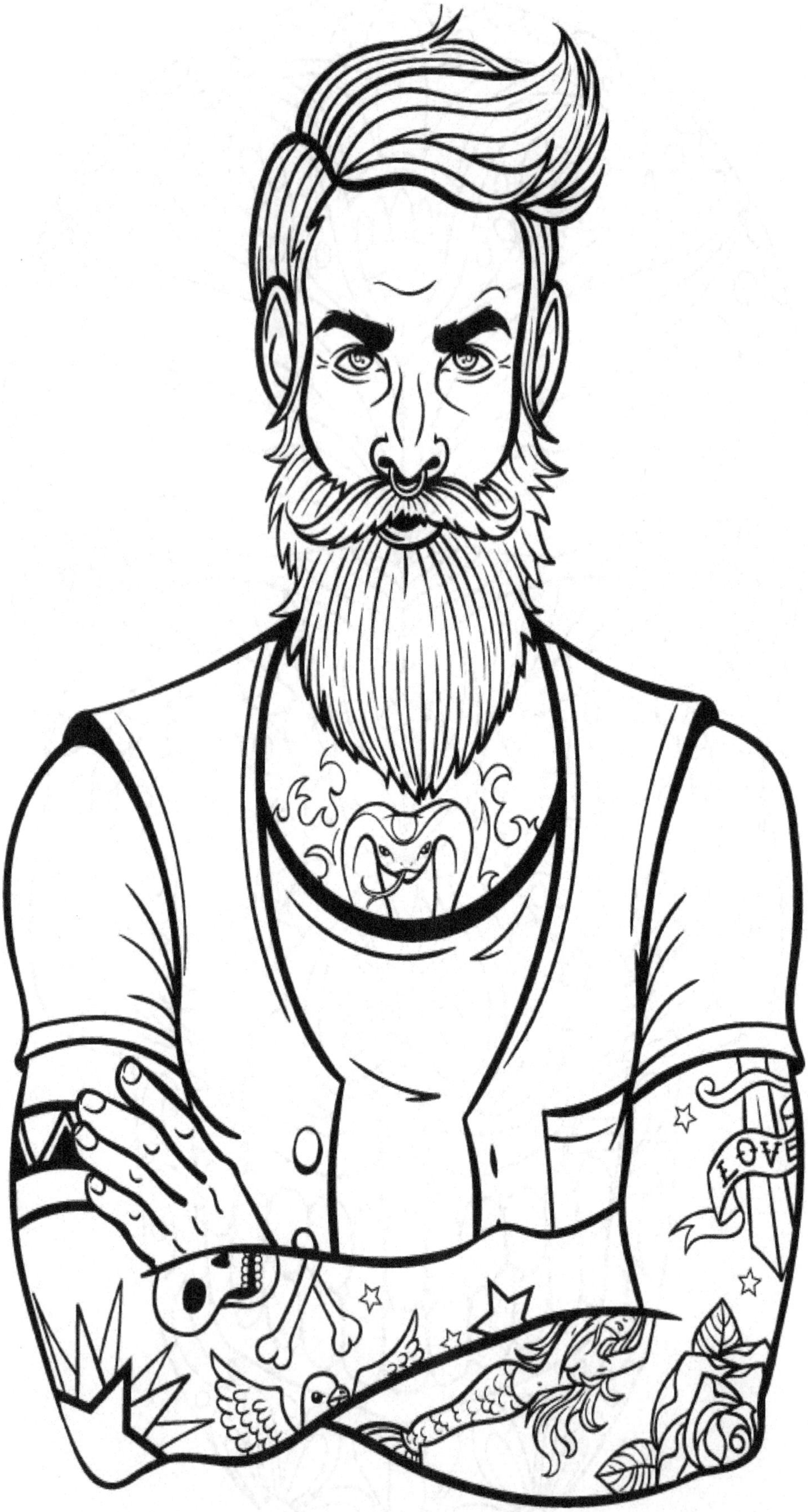
LOVE

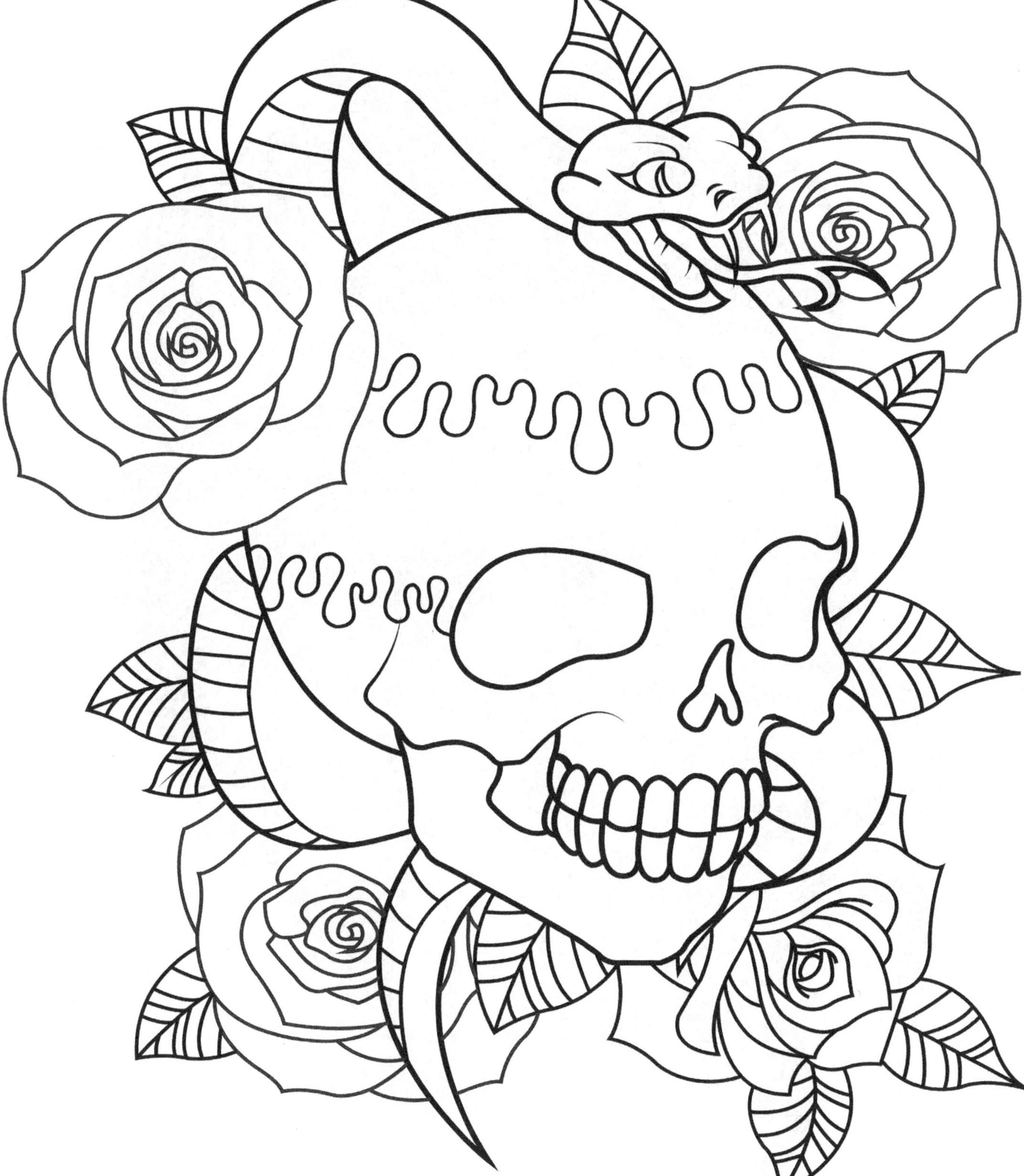

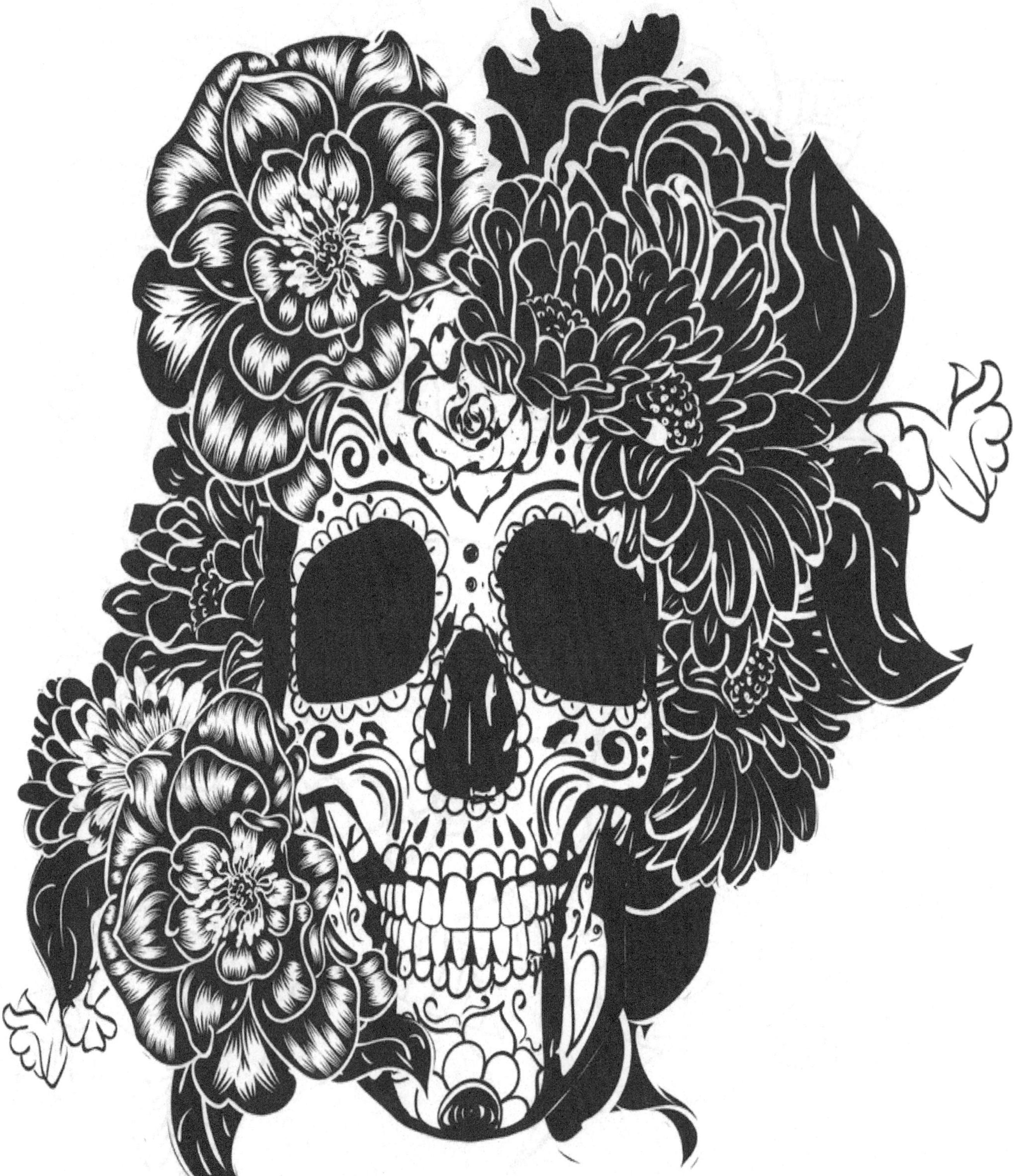

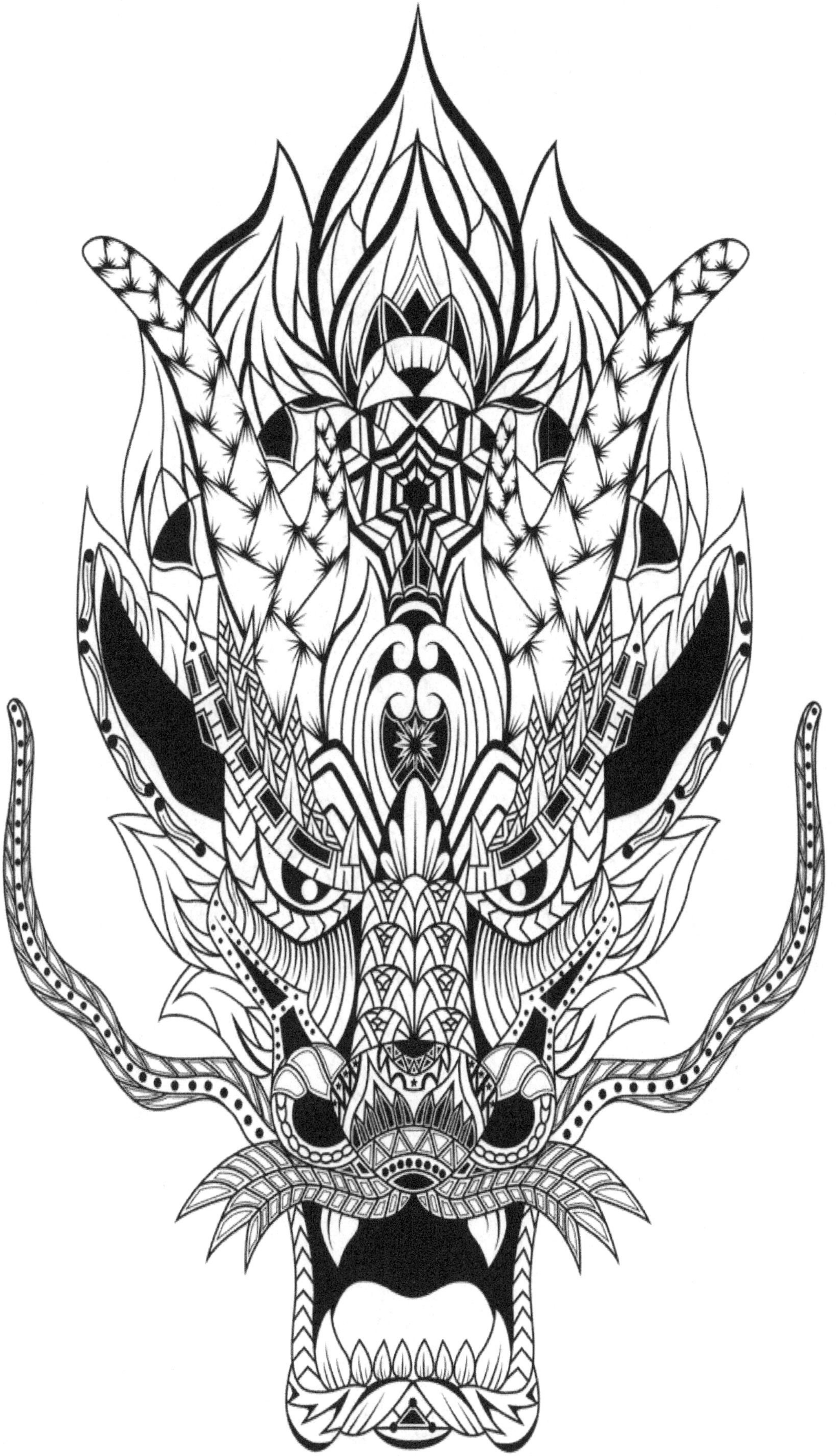

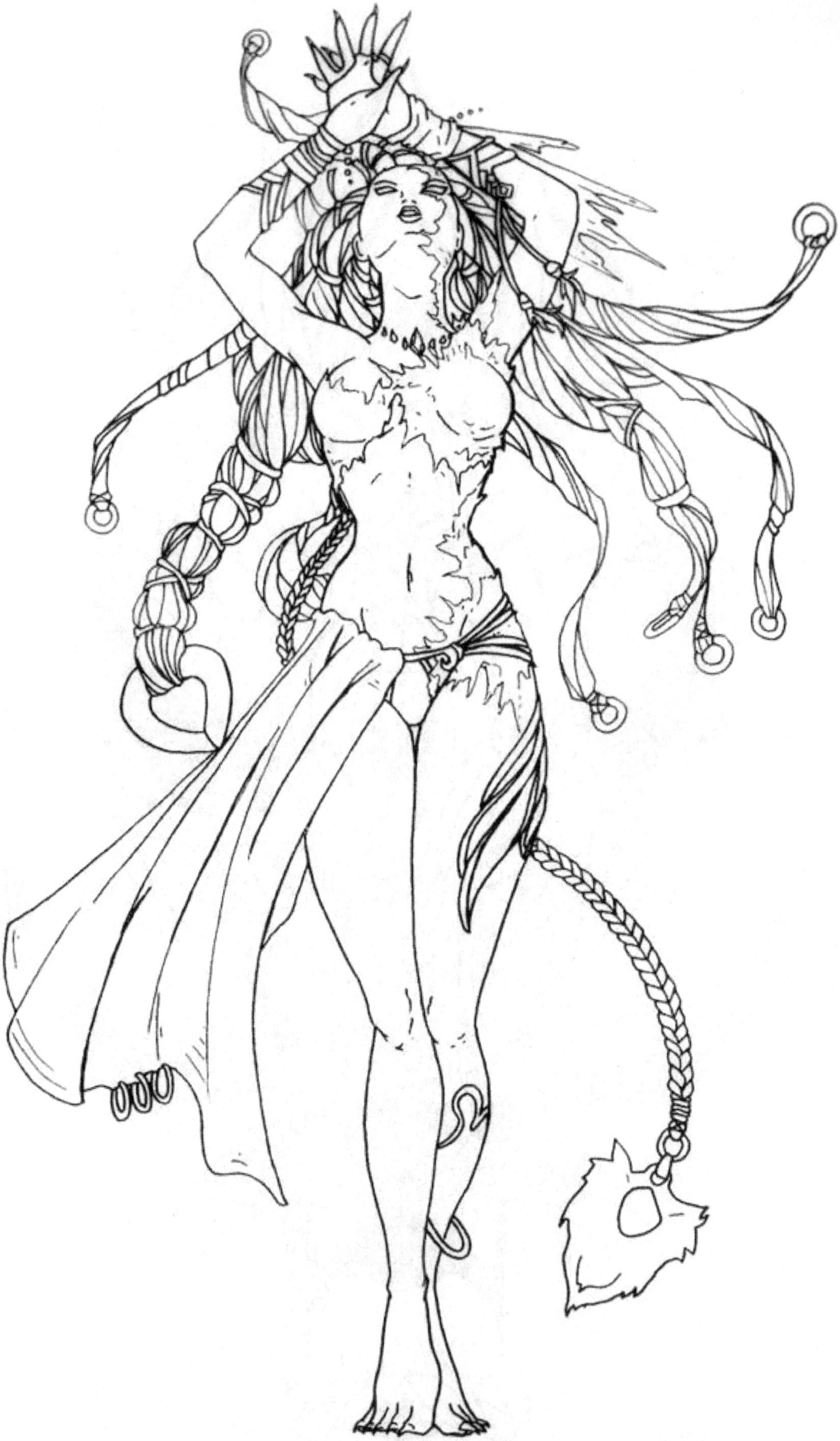

Made in the USA
Columbia, SC
25 February 2025

54397152R00037